An Introduction to Multicultural Education

FOURTH EDITION

An Introduction to Multicultural Education

James A. Banks
*University of Washington,
Seattle*

PEARSON

Boston ■ New York ■ San Francisco ■ Mexico City
Montreal ■ Toronto ■ London ■ Madrid ■ Munich ■ Paris
Hong Kong ■ Singapore ■ Tokyo ■ Cape Town ■ Sydney

Series Editor: *Kelly Villella Canton*
Editorial Assistant: *Angela Pickard*
Marketing Manager: *Weslie Sellinger*
Production Editor: *Gregory Erb*
Editorial Production Service: *Trinity Publishers Services*
Composition Buyer: *Linda Cox*
Manufacturing Buyer: *Linda Morris*
Electronic Composition: *Omegatype Typography, Inc.*
Cover Administrator: *Joel Gendron*

For related titles and support materials, visit our online catalog at
www.ablongman.com.

Between the time website information is gathered and then published, it is not
unusual for some sites to have closed. Also, the transcription of URLs can result
in typographical errors. The publisher would appreciate notification where
these errors occur so that they may be corrected in subsequent editions.

Library of Congress Cataloging-in-Publication Data

Banks, James A.
  An introduction to multicultural education / James A. Banks.—4th ed.
    p. cm.
  Includes bibliographical references and index.
  ISBN 0-205-51885-0 (pbk.)
    1. Multicultural education—United States.　I. Title.
  LC1099.3.B36 2008
  370.117—dc22

                                                        2006032820

Printed in the United States of America

10　9　8　7　6　5　4　3　2　1　CST　11　10　09　08　07

Credits appear on page 155, which constitutes an extension of the copyright
page.

For Angela and Patricia, my children
To whom the torch will pass

Contents

Preface

International population movements—which have intensified since the mid-1970s—have increased racial, ethnic, cultural, and religious diversity around the world. Diversity is enriched in Western European nations such as the United Kingdom, France, and The Netherlands by immigrants from their former colonies who are seeking to fulfill their dreams for a better life. Immigrant nations such as Brazil, Australia, Canada, and the United States have depended upon immigrants or slaves to build their nations since their founding and to make them thrive and prosper. The groups these nations have welcomed have changed with the times, but they have been immigrant nations since their inception.

Ethnic, racial, cultural, and religious diversity is increasing in the United States as well as in its schools, colleges, and universities. The United States has not experienced such massive growth in its foreign-born population since the early 1900s. The percentage of students of color in U.S. public schools doubled in the 30 years between 1973 and 2004, growing from 22 to 43 percent of the school population. If current trends continue, students of color might outnumber White students within one or two decades. Students of color already exceed the number of White students in six states: California, Hawaii, Louisiana, Mississippi, New Mexico, and Texas (Dillon, 2006).

Language and religious diversity is also increasing in U.S. schools. The largest growth in the U.S. student population in the future will be among Latinos because of their high immigration and birthrates. In 2000, 18 percent of the total U.S. population age 5 and over spoke a language other than English at home (Shin & Bruno, 2003). English language learners are the fastest-growing population in U.S. public schools. Harvard professor of religion Diane Eck (2001) calls the United States the most religiously diverse nation in the world. Islam is the fastest-growing religion in the United States as well as in several European nations, such as France and the United Kingdom.

Diversity presents both challenges and opportunities for teachers, schools, and nations. An important goal of multicultural education is to help educators to minimize the problems related to diversity and to maximize its educational opportunities and possibilities. To respond creatively and effectively to diversity, teachers and administrators need a sophisticated grasp of the concepts, principles, theories, and practices in multicultural education. They also need to examine and clarify their own racial and ethnic attitudes and to develop the pedagogical knowledge and skills necessary to work effectively with students from diverse cultural, racial, ethnic, language, and social-class groups.

An Introduction to Multicultural Education, Fourth Edition, is designed to introduce preservice and practicing educators to the major concepts, principles, theories, and practices in multicultural education. It was written for readers who can devote only limited time to the topic. Chapter 1 discusses the goals of multicultural education and the widespread misconceptions about it. Chapter 2 describes why multicultural education is essential to help students acquire the knowledge, skills, and attitudes needed to function as effective citizens in a diverse global society. This new chapter incorporates some of the concepts and insights from my most recent work on citizenship education in multicultural nation-states (Banks, 2004a). The dimensions of multicultural education and the characteristics of an effective multicultural school are discussed in Chapter 3. Chapter 4 describes the ways in which multicultural education seeks to transform the curriculum so that all students can acquire the knowledge, attitudes, and skills needed to become effective citizens in a pluralistic democratic society. The idea that multicultural education is in the shared public interest of democratic nation-states is a key tenet of this chapter.

The knowledge components needed by practicing educators to function effectively in multicultural classrooms and schools are examined in Chapters 5 and 6. The types of knowledge effective teachers need are described in Chapter 5. This chapter also describes the major paradigms, key concepts, powerful ideas, and the kinds of historical and cultural knowledge related to ethnic groups that are necessary for today's educators. Chapter 6 discusses the characteristics of multicultural lessons and units organized around powerful ideas and concepts. This chapter contains two teaching units that exemplify these characteristics.

School reform and intergroup education are discussed in Chapter 7. The need to reform U.S. schools in response to demographic changes is examined in the first part of the chapter; the second part discusses intergroup education and the nature of students' racial attitudes. Guidelines for helping students develop democratic racial attitudes and values are presented. School reform with the goals of both increasing academic achievement and helping students develop democratic racial attitudes is essential if the United States is to compete successfully in an interdependent global society and to help all students become caring, committed, and active citizens.

Chapter 8 conceptualizes multicultural education as an education for freedom, which is essential for the survival of democracy in multicultural nations at a time when democracy is being seriously challenged and eroded around the world. The spread of terrorism around the world and the responses to it pose serious challenges to democracy. Chapter 9 summarizes the book with a discussion of major benchmarks that educators can use to determine whether a school or educational institution is implementing multicultural education in its best and deepest sense.

In preparing this fourth edition of *An Introduction to Multicultural Education*, I have incorporated new developments, trends, and issues throughout the text. I have also updated the citations and references throughout the book. This edition contains two new chapters—Chapters 2 and 8. It also contains two new lessons on multicultural math and science, which are added to Chapter 6.

This book was written to provide readers with a brief, comprehensive overview of multicultural education, a grasp of its complexity, and a helpful understanding of what it means for educational practice. Readers who want to study multicultural education in greater depth will find the references and resources at the end of this book helpful, including Appendix D, A Multicultural Education Basic Library. I hope this book will start readers on an enriching path in multicultural education that will continue and deepen throughout their careers.

Acknowledgments

I would like to acknowledge the research assistance given to me by Dennis Rudnick, a research assistant in the Center for Multicultural Education at the University of Washington, in the preparation of this fourth edition. I thank Cherry A. McGee Banks for being a colleague and friend who always listens and responds with thoughtful and keen insights. I thank my colleagues in the College of Education and the Center for Multicultural Education—especially Geneva Gay, Michael S. Knapp, Walter C. Parker, Tom T. Stritikus, and Manka M. Varghese—for stimulating conversations about race, class, diversity, language, and education. These colleagues help to make the college and the center rich intellectual communities. The following reviewers offered helpful suggestions for the preparation of this fourth edition: Ronald Chennault, DePaul University; Sue Ellen Feuerstein, Bucknell University; and Pamela Lynn Martin, William Penn University.

Goals and Misconceptions

Multicultural education is a reform movement designed to make some major changes in the education of students. Multicultural education theorists and researchers believe that many school, college, and university practices related to race, ethnicity, language, and religion are harmful to students and reinforce many of the stereotypes and discriminatory practices in Western societies (Banks & Banks, 2004; Ladson-Billings & Gillborn, 2004; Modood, Triandafyllidou, & Zapata-Barrero, 2006).

Multicultural education assumes that race, ethnicity, culture, religion, and social class are salient parts of the United States and other Western nations. It also assumes that diversity enriches a nation and increases the ways in which its citizens can perceive and solve personal and public problems. Diversity also enriches a nation by providing all citizens with rich opportunities to experience other cultures and thus to become more fulfilled as human beings. When individuals are able to participate in a variety of cultures, they are more able to benefit from the total human experience.

The Goals of Multicultural Education

Individuals who know the world only from their own cultural perspectives are denied important parts of the human experience and are culturally and ethnically encapsulated. These individuals are also unable to know their own cultures fully because of their cultural blinders. We can get a full view of our own backgrounds and behaviors only by viewing them from the perspectives of other cultures. Just as fish are unable to appreciate the uniqueness of their aquatic environment, so are many mainstream individuals and groups within a society unable to fully see and appreciate the uniqueness of their cultural characteristics. A key goal of multicultural education is to help individuals gain greater self-understanding by viewing themselves from the perspectives of other cultures. Multicultural education assumes that with acquaintance and understanding, respect may follow.

Another major goal of multicultural education is to provide students with cultural, ethnic, and language alternatives. Historically, the school curriculum in the United States and other Western nations has focused primarily on the cultures and histories of mainstream groups with power and influence. The school culture and curriculum in the United States were primarily extensions of the culture of mainstream Anglo American students (Graham, 2005). The school rarely presented mainstream students with cultural and ethnic alternatives.

The Anglocentric curriculum, which still exists to varying degrees in U.S. schools, colleges, and universities, has harmful consequences for both mainstream Anglo American students and students of color, such as African Americans and Mexican Americans (Nussbaum, 1997). By teaching mainstream students only about their own cultures, the school is denying them the richness of the music, literature, values, lifestyles, and perspectives of such ethnic groups as African Americans, Puerto Rican Americans, and Polish Americans. Mainstream American students should know that African American literature is uniquely enriching (Gates & McKay, 1997) and that groups such as Italian Americans and Mexican Americans have values they can embrace.

The Anglocentric curriculum negatively affects many students of color because they often find the school culture alien, hostile, and self-defeating. Because of the negative ways in which students of color and their cultures are often viewed by educators and the negative experiences of these students in their communities and in the schools, many of them do not attain the skills needed to function successfully in a highly technological, knowledge-oriented society (Anyon, 2005; Conchas, 2006; Lipman, 2004; Tomlinson, 2001).

A major goal of multicultural education is to provide all students with the skills, attitudes, and knowledge needed to function within their community cultures, within the mainstream culture, and within and across other ethnic cultures (Banks, 2006b). Mainstream American students should have a sophisticated understanding and appreciation for the uniqueness and richness of Black English (also called Ebonics, which is formed from the words ebony and phonics). African American students should be able to speak and write standard English and to function successfully within mainstream institutions without experiencing cultural alienation from family and community (Delpit & Dowdy, 2002). The widespread misunderstandings and misconceptions about Ebonics among Americans within many groups became acutely evident when a controversy about it arose in the Oakland (California) Public Schools during the 1996–1997 school year.

Another major goal of multicultural education is to reduce the pain and discrimination that members of some ethnic and racial groups experience because of their unique racial, physical, and cultural characteristics. Filipino Americans, Mexican Americans, Puerto Rican Americans, and Chinese Americans often deny their ethnic identity, ethnic heritage, and family in order to assimilate and participate more fully in mainstream institutions (Alba & Nee, 2003). Jewish Americans, Polish Americans, and Italian Americans also frequently reject parts of their ethnic cultures when trying to succeed in school and in mainstream society (Brodkin, 1998; Jacobson, 1998). As Dickeman (1973) has insightfully pointed out, schools often force members of these groups to experience "self-alienation" in order to succeed. Wong Fillmore (2005) describes how the school alienates immigrant children from their families when it forces them to give up their home language. These are high prices to pay for educational, social, and economic mobility. Students who become successful in school and in the larger society but become alienated from self, family, and community experience what Fordham (1988) has called a "pyrrhic victory"—a victory with pain and losses.

Some individuals of color in the United States—such as many African Americans, Native Americans, and Puerto Rican Americans—in their effort to assimilate and to participate fully in mainstream institutions, become very Anglo-Saxon in their ways of viewing the world and in their values and behavior. However, highly culturally assimilated members of ethnic groups of color are often denied full participation in mainstream institutions because of their skin color (Cose, 1993; Delgado, 1995; Feagin & Sikes, 1994). These individuals may also become alienated from their community cultures and families in their attempts to fully participate in mainstream institutions. They may become alienated from both their community cultures and mainstream society and consequently experience marginality.

Jewish Americans and Italian Americans may also experience marginality when they deny their cultures in an attempt to become fully assimilated into American mainstream society and culture (Dershowitz, 1997). Although they usually succeed in looking and acting like Anglo Americans, they are likely to experience psychological stress and identity conflict when they deny and reject their family and their ethnic languages, symbols, behaviors, and beliefs (Brodkin, 1998). Ethnicity plays a major role in the socialization of many members of ethnic groups; ethnic identity is an important part of the identity of such individuals (Appiah, 2006; Gutmann, 2003). When these individuals deny their ethnic cultures and identities, they reject an important part of self.

It is important for educators to realize that ethnic group membership is not an important part of personal identity for many individual members of ethnic groups. Other group affiliations, such as religion, social class, gender, or sexual orientation, are more important identities for these individuals. Some people identify with more than one ethnic or cultural group (Heath & McLaughlin, 1993). This is especially likely to be the case for individuals who are racially and ethnically mixed—an increasing population within American society (Wardle & Cruz-Janzen, 2004; Root & Kelley, 2003). Ethnic identity becomes complicated for individuals of color for whom ethnic identity is not significant. Even though such individuals may not view their ethnic group membership as important, other people, especially those within other racial and ethnic groups, may view these individuals as members of a racial/ethnic group and think that ethnicity is their primary identity.

Ethnic group members who experience marginality are likely to be alienated citizens who feel that they have little stake in society (Modood, Triandafyllidou, & Zapata-Barrero, 2006). Those who reject their basic group identity are incapable of becoming fully functioning and self-actualized citizens and are more likely to experience political and social alienation. It thus is in the best interests of a political democracy to protect the rights of all citizens to maintain allegiances to their ethnic and cultural groups (Banks, 2004; Castles, 2004; Kymlicka, 1995). Individuals are capable of maintaining allegiance both to their ethnic group and to the nation-state (Banks, 1997).

Another goal of multicultural education is to help students to acquire the reading, writing, and math skills needed to function effectively in a global and "flat" technological world—that is, one in which students in New York City, London, Paris, and Berlin must compete for jobs with students educated in developing nations such as India and Pakistan (Friedman, 2005). Technology enables companies to outsource jobs to developing nations to reduce the costs of products and services. Multicultural education assumes that multicultural content can help students to master basic skills essential to function in a global and flat world. Providing multicultural readings and data can be highly motivating and meaningful for students (Lee, 2007). Students are more likely to master skills when the teacher uses content that deals with significant human problems related to race, ethnicity, and social class within society. Students around the world, including American students, live in societies in which ethnic, racial, language, and religious problems are real and salient. Providing content related to these issues and to the cultural communities in which students live is significant and meaningful to students. Multicultural education theorists and researchers maintain that skill goals are extremely important.

Education within a pluralistic society should affirm and help students understand their home and community cultures. It should also help free them from their cultural boundaries. To create and maintain a civic community that works for the common good, education in a democratic society should help students acquire the knowledge, attitudes, and skills needed to participate in civic action to make society more equitable and just.

Education and Global Citizenship

Another important goal of multicultural education is to help individuals from diverse racial, cultural, language, and religion groups to acquire the knowledge, attitudes, and skills needed to function effectively within their cultural communities, the national civic culture, their regional culture, and the global community (Banks, 2004). In the past, most nation-states required citizens to experience cultural assimilation into the national culture and to become alienated from their community cultures in order to become citizens. The assimilationist conception of citizenship and citizenship education have come into question in view of the historical, political, social, and cultural developments that have occurred around the world since World War II. Institutionalized notions of citizenship have been vigorously contested since the ethnic revitalization movements starting in the 1960s and 1970s. Worldwide immigration, the challenges to nation-states brought by globalization, and the tenacity of nationalism and national borders have stimulated debate, controversy, and rethinking about citizenship and citizenship education (Castles & Davidson, 2000; Benhabib, 2004).

Traditional notions of citizenship assume that individuals from different groups had to give up their homes and community cultures and languages in order to attain inclusion and participate effectively in the national civic culture. Assimilationist conceptions of citizenship education need to be questioned. Citizenship education needs to be expanded to include cultural rights for citizens from diverse racial, cultural, ethnic, language, and religious groups (Young, 2000).

An effective citizenship education helps students to acquire the knowledge, skills, and values needed to function effectively within their cultural communities, nation-states, regions, and the global community. Such an education helps students acquire the cosmopolitan perspectives and values needed to work to attain equality and social justice for people around the world (Nussbaum, 2002). Schools should be reformed so that they can implement a transformative and critical conception of citizenship education that will enhance educational equality for all students.

No Child Left Behind and the Standardization Movement

The No Child Left Behind Act was enacted by the U.S. Congress in 2001 and signed by President George W. Bush in 2002 to address the academic achievement gap between White students and students of color. One of the stated goals of the act is to make school districts and states accountable for the academic achievement of students from diverse racial, ethnic, and language groups. The act requires states to formulate rigorous standards in reading and mathematics and to annually test all students in grades 3 through 8 in these subjects. Science is now being added to the subjects that are required to be tested. The act also requires that the results of the assessments be disaggregated by income, race, ethnicity, disability, and limited English proficiency (Guthrie, 2003).

Many of the standards-based school reforms were created to respond to the requirements of the No Child Left Behind Act (NCLB). However, many states had initiated standards-based reforms prior to the passage of NCLB. The national focus on creating high academic standards and holding educators accountable for student achievement is having mixed results in the nation's schools. Some researchers and educational leaders view the reforms required by NCLB as promising. A study by Roderick, Jacob, and Bryk (2002) indicates that performance improved in low-performing schools after the implementation of standards-based reform. Some school leaders in high-minority, low-achieving schools have applauded NCLB because it requires school districts and states to disaggregate achievement data by income, race, ethnicity, disability, and limited English proficiency. These administrators believe that the disaggregation of achievement data has helped to focus attention on the academic achievement gap between White students and students of color such as African Americans, Mexican Americans, and Native Americans.

The NCLB and related reforms have evoked a chorus of criticism from other researchers and school reformers (Meier & Wood, 2005). The critics of the act argue that standards-based reforms driven by NCLB have had many negative consequences on the curriculum and on school life. They contend that these reforms have forced many teachers to focus on narrow literacy and numeracy skills rather than on critical thinking and the broad goals of schooling in a democratic society. In addition, concerns are voiced about an overemphasis on testing, less focus on teaching, and deskilled (Giroux, 1988) and deprofessionalized teachers.

Amrein and Berliner (2002) analyzed 18 states to determine how high-stakes tests were affecting student learning. They concluded that in all but one of their analyses, student learning was indeterminate, remained at the same level before high-stakes testing was implemented, or went down when high-stakes testing policies were initiated.

Sleeter (2005) makes an important distinction between *standards* and *standardization* and explains why she supports standards but is opposed to standardization. Standards—which describe quality—can be used by teachers to help students attain high levels of academic achievement. Standardization has negative effects on students, teachers, and schools because it leads to bureaucratization and to a focus on low-level knowledge and skills that can be easily measured by norm-referenced tests.

Teachers face a dilemma when they try to teach in culturally responsive ways as well as help students acquire the knowledge and skills needed to perform successfully on state and national standardized tests. If teachers ignore the tests, low-achieving students will become further marginalized within schools and society and the existing social, political, and economic structures will be perpetuated (Willis, 1977). Teachers may also put their own professional reputations and status at risk because of punitive sanctions they can experience in many school districts if the test scores of their students do not increase between testing cycles.

Sleeter (2005) recommends that teachers use multicultural content—which is highly motivating to students when it focuses on their own historical and cultural experience—to help students from diverse groups attain the knowledge and skills needed to reach high levels of achievement on standardized tests. At the same time, teachers should help students conceptualize actions they can take to change the political, economic, and social systems that have victimized their groups historically and that still victimize them today (Baldwin, 1985; Banks, 2006c; Freire, 2000).

The Multicultural Debate

Multicultural education is an education for freedom that is essential in today's ethnically polarized and troubled world (Parekh, 2006). During the early 1990s, multicultural education evoked a divisive national debate, in part because of the divergent views that citizens hold about what constitutes an American identity and about the roots and nature of American civilization. In turn, the debate sparked a power struggle over who should participate in formulating the canon used to shape the curriculum in the nation's schools, colleges, and universities (Cain, 1994; Nussbaum, 1997).

During the 1990s, the bitter canon debate in the popular press and in several widely reviewed books overshadowed the progress in multicultural education that had been made since the Civil Rights movement of the 1960s and 1970s. The debate also perpetuated harmful misconceptions about theory and practice in multicultural education. It consequently increased racial and ethnic tension and trivialized the field's remarkable accomplishments in theory, research, and curriculum development. The truth about the development and attainments of multicultural education needs to be told, for the sake of balance, scholarly integrity, and accuracy.

Misconceptions

Multicultural Education Is for the Others

To reveal the truth about multicultural education, some of the frequently repeated and widespread myths and misconceptions about it must be identified and debunked. One such misconception is that multicultural education is an entitlement program and curriculum movement for African Americans, Latinos, the poor, women, and other marginalized groups (D'Souza, 1991; Glazer, 1997; Leo, 2000).

The major theorists and researchers in multicultural education agree that it is a reform movement designed to restructure educational institutions so that all students, including White, male, and middle-class students, will acquire the knowledge, skills, and attitudes needed to function effectively in a culturally and ethnically diverse nation and world (Banks & Banks, 2004; Ladson-Billings, 2004; Nieto, 2004). Multicultural education, as defined and conceptualized by its major architects during the last decade, is not an ethnic- or gender-specific movement, but a movement designed to empower all students to become knowledgeable, caring, and active citizens in a deeply troubled and ethnically polarized nation and world.

The claim that multicultural education is only for ethnic groups of color and the disenfranchised is one of the most pernicious and damaging misconceptions with which the movement has to cope (Glazer, 1997). It has caused serious problems and has haunted the multicultural education movement since its inception. Despite everything written and spoken about multicultural education being for all students, the image of multicultural education as an entitlement program for the "others" remains strong and vivid in the public imagination as well as in the hearts and minds of many teachers and administrators. Teachers who teach in predominantly White schools and districts often state that they don't have a program or plan for multicultural education because they have few African American, Latino, or Asian American students.

When multicultural education is viewed by educators as the study of the "other," it is marginalized and prevented from becoming a part of mainstream educational reform. Several critics of multicultural education, such as Schlesinger (1991), Glazer (1997), and Gray (1991), have perpetuated the idea that multicultural education is the study of the "other" by defining it as the same as Afrocentric education.

The history of intergroup education teaches us that only when educational reform related to diversity is viewed as essential for all students— and as promoting the broad public interest—will it have a reasonable chance of becoming institutionalized in the nation's schools, colleges, and universities (C. A. M. Banks, 2005). The intergroup education movement of the 1940s and 1950s failed in large part because intergroup educators were never able to get mainstream educators to believe that it was needed by and designed for all students (Taba, Brady, & Robinson, 1952). To its bitter and quiet end, intergroup education was viewed as something for schools with racial problems and as something for "them" and not for "us."

Multicultural Education Is Against the West

Another harmful misconception about multicultural education has been repeated so often by its critics that it is frequently viewed by readers as self-evident. This is the claim that multicultural education is a movement against the West and Western civilization. Multicultural education is not against the West because most writers of color—such as Rudolfo A. Anaya, Paula Gunn Allen, N. Scott Momaday, Maxine Hong Kingston, Maya Angelou, and Toni Morrison—are Western. Multicultural education itself is a thoroughly Western movement. It grew out of a Civil Rights movement grounded in Western democratic ideals such as freedom, justice, and equality. Multicultural education seeks to expand for all people ideals that were meant for an elite few at the nation's beginning (Foner, 1998; Franklin, 2005).

Although multicultural education is not against the West, its theorists believe that the truth about the West should be told, that its debt to people of color and women be recognized and included in the curriculum, and that the discrepancies between the ideals of freedom and equality and the realities of racism and sexism be taught to students. Reflective citizen action is also an integral part of multicultural theory. Multicultural education views citizen action to improve society as an integral part of education in a democracy. It links knowledge, values, empowerment, and action (Banks, 1996a, b; 2006c). Multicultural education is postmodern in its assumptions about knowledge and knowledge construction. It challenges Enlightenment, positivist assumptions about the relationship between human values, knowledge, and action.

Positivists, who are heirs of the Enlightenment, believe that it is possible to structure knowledge that is objective and beyond human values and interests. Multicultural theorists maintain that knowledge is positional, that it relates to the knower's values and experiences, and that knowledge implies action (Harding, 1998). Consequently, different concepts, theories, and paradigms imply different kinds of actions. Multicultural theorists believe that in order to have valid knowledge, information about the social condition and experiences of the knower is essential (Code, 1991; Collins, 2000).

A few critics of multicultural education, such as Leo (2000) and D'Souza (1991), claim that multicultural education has reduced or displaced the study of Western civilization in the nation's schools, colleges, and universities. When this claim was made, Gerald Graff (1992) pointed out in his informative book, *Beyond the Cultural Wars*, that it simply was not true. Graff cited research by himself at the college level and by Applebee (1993) at the high school level to substantiate his conclusion that European and American male authors such as Shakespeare, Dante, Chaucer, Twain, and Hemingway still dominated the required reading lists in the nation's high schools, colleges, and universities. Graff found that most of the books by authors of color in the cases he examined were optional rather than required readings. Applebee found that of the ten most frequently assigned, required book-length works taught in the high school grades, only one title was by a female author (Harper Lee, *To Kill a Mockingbird*), and none was by a writer of color. Works by Shakespeare, Steinbeck, and Dickens lead the list. Although the studies by Graff and Applebee were completed more than ten years ago, there is little reason to believe that the books that students are reading in high school English classes are very different today.

Multicultural Education Will Divide the Nation

Many of its critics claim that multicultural education will divide the nation and undercut its unity. Schlesinger (1991) underscores this view by titling his book *The Disuniting of America: Reflections on a Multicultural Society*. This misconception of multicultural education is based partly on questionable assumptions about the nature of U.S. society and partly on a mistaken view about multicultural education. The claim that multicultural education will divide the nation assumes that the nation is already united. While we are one nation politically, sociologically our nation is deeply divided along racial, gender, sexual orientation, and class lines. Class is one of the most pernicious divisions in the United States; the gap between the classes is widening. The percentage of the nation's wealth owned by the top 1 percent of Americans increased from 20 percent in 1976 to 47 percent in 2001 (DeNavas-Walt, Procter, & Lee, 2005).

Multicultural education is designed to help unify a deeply divided nation rather than to divide a highly cohesive one. Multicultural education supports the notion of *e pluribus unum*—one out of many. The multiculturalists and the Western traditionalists, however, often differ about how the *unum* can best be attained. Traditionally, the larger U.S. society as well as the schools have tried to create the *unum* by assimilating students from diverse racial and ethnic groups into a mythical Anglo American culture that required them to experience a process of self-alienation and harsh assimilation. However, even when students of color became culturally assimilated, they were often structurally excluded from mainstream institutions.

Multicultural educators view *e pluribus unum* as the appropriate national goal but believe that the goal must be negotiated, discussed, and restructured to reflect a nation's ethnic, cultural, language, and religious diversity. The reformulation of the *unum* must be a process and must involve the participation by diverse groups within the nation, such as people of color, women, straights, gays, the powerful, the powerless, the young, and the old. The reformulation of the *unum* must also involve power sharing and participation by people from many different cultural communities. They must discuss, debate, share power, experience equal status, and reach beyond their cultural and ethnic borders in order to create a common civic culture that reflects and contributes to the well-being of all. This common civic culture will extend beyond the cultural borders of each group and constitute a civic borderland culture.

In *Borderlands,* Gloria Anzaldua (1999) contrasts cultural *borders* and *borderlands*. She states the need to weaken cultural borders and to create a shared borderland culture in which people from many different cultures can interact, relate, and engage in civic talk and action. Anzaldua states that "borders are set up to define the places that are safe and unsafe, to distinguish us from them. A border is a dividing line, a narrow strip along a steep edge. A borderland is a vague and undetermined place created by the residue of an unnatural boundary. It is in a constant state of transition" (p. 3).

Progress in Multicultural Education

Multicultural Education Has Made Significant Curriculum Inroads

While it is still not the center of the curriculum in many schools, colleges, and universities, multicultural content and perspectives have made significant inroads into both the school and the higher education curriculum within the last four decades. The truth lies somewhere between the claim that no progress has been made in infusing and transforming the school and college curriculum with multicultural content and the claim that such content has replaced the European and American classics.

In the elementary and high schools, much more ethnic content appears in social studies and language arts textbooks today than was the case 10 or 20 years ago. Also, some teachers assign works written by authors of color along with the more standard American classics. More classroom teachers today have studied multicultural education concepts than at any previous point in U.S. history. A significant percentage of today's classroom teachers took a required teacher education course in multicultural education when they were in college. The multicultural education standard adopted by the National Council for the Accreditation of Teacher Education (NCATE) in 1977—which became effective January 1, 1979—was a major factor that stimulated the growth of multicultural education in teacher education programs. The NCATE diversity standard (standard 4) states: "The unit designs, implements and evaluates curriculum and experiences for candidates to acquire and apply the knowledge, skills and dispositions necessary to help all students learn. These experiences include working with diverse higher education faculty and school faculty, diverse candidates, and diverse students in P–12 schools" (NCATE 2006, p. 29). In commenting on the diversity standard, NCATE (2006) gives examples of the behaviors expected of teacher education programs and candidates that meet it:

> Candidates learn to develop and teach lessons that incorporate diversity and develop a classroom and school climate that values diversity. Candidates become aware of different teaching and learning styles shaped by cultural influences and are able to adapt instruction and services appropriately for all students, including students with exceptionalities. (p. 29)

The teacher education market in multicultural education textbooks is now a substantial one. Most major publishers currently publish several major college textbooks in the field. Most major textbooks in other required education courses—such as educational psychology and the foundations of education—have separate chapters or sections that examine concepts and developments in multicultural education. Some of the nation's leading colleges and universities—such as the University of California, Berkeley; the University of Minnesota–Twin Cities; and Stanford University—have either revised their core to include ethnic content or have established an ethnic studies course requirement.

However, the transformation of the traditional canon on college and university campuses has often been bitter and divisive. All curriculum changes come slowly and painfully to university campuses (Nussbaum, 1997). The linkage of curriculum change with issues related to race evokes latent primordial feelings and reflects the racial crisis in Western societies, including the United States. On some campuses—such as the University of Washington, Seattle—a bitter struggle ended with the defeat of the ethnic studies requirement. Ironically, the undergraduate population of students of color at the University of Washington is increasing substantially. In spring 2006, they made up 34.96 percent of the Washington undergraduate population, most of whom were Asian Americans (25.62 percent) (University of Washington, 2006).

Changes are also coming to elementary and high school textbooks. The demographic imperative is an important factor driving the changes in school textbooks. The color of the nation's students is changing rapidly. In 2003, 42 percent of the nation's public elementary and secondary students were students of color (NCES, 2006a). Table 1.1 shows the enrollment in public elementary and secondary schools by race or ethnicity in 1986, 2000, and 2003. It is projected that nearly half (about 45.5 percent) of the nation's school-age youth will be youth of color by 2020 (Pallas, Natriello, & McDill, 1989).

Language diversity is also increasing in the United States. In 2000 18 percent of Americans—or 47 million—spoke a language at home other than English (U.S. Census Bureau, 2000). Table 1.2. shows the twenty most frequently spoken languages at home other than English by people who live in the United States. Parents of color and parents who speak a first language other than English are demanding that their leaders,

TABLE 1.1   Enrollment in Public Elementary and Secondary Schools, by Race and Ethnicity, Fall 1986, 1999–2000 School Year, and Fall 2003 (percentage distribution)

Group	Fall 1986	1999–2000	Fall 2003
White	70.4	62.1	58.7
Black	16.1	17.2	17.2
Hispanic	9.9	15.6	18.5
Asian or Pacific Islander	2.8	4.0	4.4
American Indian/Alaskan Native	.09	1.2	1.2

Sources: National Center for Education Statistics (2001, 2006a); U.S. Department of Education (1993, 2003).

TABLE 1.2   Twenty Languages Most Frequently Spoken at Home for the
Population Ages 5 Years and Over, 1990 and 2000

Language spoken at home	1990		2000	
	Rank	Number of speakers	Rank	Total
United States	(X)	230,445,777	(X)	262,375,152
English only	(X)	198,600,798	(X)	215,423,557
Total non-English	(X)	31,844,979	(X)	46,951,595
Spanish	1	17,339,172	1	28,101,052
Chinese	5	1,249,213	2	2,022,143
French	2	1,702,176	3	1,643,838
German	3	1,547,099	4	1,382,613
Tagalog	6	843,251	5	1,224,241
Vietnamese[1]	9	507,069	6	1,009,627
Italian[1]	4	1,308,648	7	1,008,370
Korean	8	626,478	8	894,063
Russian	15	241,798	9	706,242
Polish	7	723,483	10	667,414
Arabic	13	355,150	11	614,582
Portuguese[2]	10	429,860	12	564,630
Japanese[2]	11	427,657	13	477,997
French Creole	19	187,658	14	453,368
Greek	12	388,260	15	365,436
Hindi[3]	14	331,484	16	317,057
Persian	18	201,865	17	312,085
Urdu[3]	(NA)	(NA)	18	262,900
Gujarathi	26	102,418	19	235,988
Armenian	20	149,694	20	202,708
All other languages	(X)	3,182,546	(X)	4,485,241

NA Not available.   X Not applicable.

[1] In 2000, the number of Vietnamese speakers and the number of Italian speakers were not statistically different from one another.
[2] In 1990, the number of Portuguese speakers and the number of Japanese speakers were not statistically different from one another.
[3] In 1990, Hindi included those who spoke Urdu.

Note: The estimates in this table vary from actual values due to sampling errors. As a result, the number of speakers of some languages shown in this table may not be statistically different from the number of speakers of languages not shown in this table.

Source: U.S. Census Bureau (2003).

images, hopes, and dreams be mirrored in the textbooks that their children study in school.

Textbooks have always reflected the myths, hopes, and dreams of the people in society with money and power. As African Americans, Latinos, Asians, and women become more influential participants on the power stage, textbooks will increasingly reflect their hopes, dreams, and disappointments. Textbooks will have to survive in the marketplace of a browner America. Because textbooks still carry the curriculum in U.S. public schools, they will remain an important focus for multicultural curriculum reformers.

Multicultural Education and the Future

The attainments of multicultural education since the late 1960s and early 1970s are noteworthy and should be acknowledged. Its shapers have been able to establish goals, aims, and approaches on which there is a high level of agreement (Banks & Banks, 2004). Most multicultural education theorists agree that the major goal of multicultural education is to restructure schools, colleges, and universities so that all students will acquire the knowledge, attitudes, and skills needed to function in an ethnically and racially diverse nation and world. As in other interdisciplinary fields of study—such as social studies, leadership, and special education—there are internal debates within the field. These debates are consistent with a field that values democracy and diversity and are also a source of strength.

Multicultural education is experiencing impressive success in being implemented in the nation's schools, colleges, and universities. The number of national conferences, school district workshops, and teacher education courses in multicultural education are evidence of its success and perceived importance. It is increasingly becoming institutionalized in educational institutions in nations such as the United States, Canada, Australia, and the United Kingdom (Banks & Banks, 2004). Although the process is slow and sometimes contentious, multicultural content is increasingly becoming a part of core courses in school, college, and university courses. Textbook publishers are also integrating their books with ethnic and cultural content and perspectives.

Despite its impressive successes, multicultural education faces important opportunities and challenges. The debate about diversity reflects the value dilemma and identity crisis in United States society. The American identity is being reshaped as groups on the margins of society begin to participate in the center and to demand that their visions be reflected in a transformed America. The power sharing and identity transformation required to make racial peace may be valued rather than feared in the future because of the contributions these groups will make to our national and global salvation.

As the ethnic texture of nations such as the United States, Canada, France, and the United Kingdom continues to deepen, educational programs related to ethnic and cultural diversity will continue to emerge and will take various shapes and forms (Banks & Banks, 2004; Modood, Triandafyllidou, & Zapata-Barrero, 2006; Tomlinson, 2001). New challenges will continue to evolve in pluralistic democratic societies. The extent to which these challenges will be transformed into opportunities will depend largely on the vision, knowledge, and commitment of each nation's educators. You will have to take a stand on multicultural education and determine what actions related to it you will take in your classroom and school. The chapters in this book are designed to help you conceptualize and take informed and reflective actions that will make your school a more caring and humane place for all students.

2

Citizenship Education and Diversity in a Global Age

In nation-states throughout the world, there is increasing diversity as well as increasing recognition of diversity. After World War II, large numbers of people from former colonies in Asia and the West Indies immigrated to the United Kingdom to improve their economic status. Since the late 1960s, Canada, Germany, France, and The Netherlands have experienced an increase in racial, cultural, language, religious, and ethnic diversity when thousands of people seeking better economic opportunities emigrated to these nations (Castles & Davidson, 2000; Douglass & Roberts, 2000; Luchtenberg, 2004; Statistics Canada, 2000). Australia and Japan also experienced an increase in racial, cultural, language, religious, and ethnic diversity when thousands of people—who were seeking better economic opportunities—emigrated to those nations (Castles & Davidson, 2000; Douglass & Roberts, 2000; Hoff, 2001; Moodley, 2001).

Although the United States has been diverse since its founding, its ethnic texture has changed dramatically since 1965 when the Immigration Reform Act was enacted. In the late 19th and early 20th centuries, most immigrants to the United States came from Europe; today, most come from nations in Asia, Latin America, and the Caribbean. Large numbers of immigrants are now entering from Mexico, the Caribbean, the Philippines, China, Korea, and India. The United States is now experiencing its largest influx of immigrants since the early 1900s (U.S. Census Bureau, 2000).

17

The U.S. Census (2000) estimates that ethnic minorities made up 28 percent of the nation's population in 2000 and predicts that they will make up 38 percent in 2025 and 50 percent in 2050. Forty-three percent of the students enrolled in U.S. public schools in 2004 were ethnic minorities (Dillon, 2006). This percentage is increasing each year, primarily because of the growth in the percentage of Latino students (NCES, 2006; Martinez & Curry, 1998). Language diversity is also increasing in the U.S. student population (August & Shanahan, 2006). In 2000, about 20 percent of the school-age population spoke a language at home other than English (U.S. Census Bureau, 2000).

Religious diversity is increasing in the United States and in other nations around the world. Writes Diana Eck (2001), Harvard professor of comparative religion and Indian studies, "The United States is the most religiously diverse nation on earth" (p. 4). The fastest-growing religion in the United States is Islam. Almost half of the growth in Islam in the United States is from converts; the majority of these converts are African Americans (Cesari, 2004). Most Muslims in the United States come from a variety of countries and ethnic groups (Cesari, 2004).

Religion is a major issue in Europe and has become an increasingly divisive issue since 9/11 and other terrorist activities by extremist Muslim groups. Muslims make up the "largest religious minority in Europe" (Cesari, 2004, p. 9). France, Germany, the United Kingdom, The Netherlands, and Greece have significant Muslim populations (Cesari, 2004; Modood, Triandafyllidou, & Zapata-Barrero, 2006). Because of the terrorist activities by groups of Muslim extremists, Islamophobia has increased in nations throughout Western Europe, including in France, the United Kingdom, and The Netherlands (Stone, 2004; King, 2006).

Increasing World Diversity and Citizenship Education

The quests for rights by ethnic minority groups that intensified in the 1960s and 1970s, the increase in international migration, the tightening of national borders, and the growth in the number of nation-states raise complex questions about diversity and citizenship education in a global world. The number of recognized nation-states increased from 43 in 1900 to approximately 190 in 2000. The number of people living outside their country of birth or citizenship grew from 120 million in 1990 to 160 million in 2000 (Martin & Widgren, 2002).

The growth in international migration, the increasing recognition of structural inequality within democratic nation-states, and the growing recognition and legitimacy of international human rights have raised complex issues related to citizenship and citizenship education in nation-states around the world, and especially in the Western democracies. The Western world is perplexed, exhausted, and fear ridden as it attempts to envision and implement viable and creative strategies to respond effectively to the conflicts in the Middle East, Islamic fundamentalism, and ethnic protest and violence in their own societies (Modood, Triandafyllidou, & Zapata-Barrero, 2006).

These events have resulted in bombings that have created a reign of terror throughout the world—including the bombing of the Pentagon and the World Trade Center on September 11, 2001; the bombings of four commuter trains in Madrid, Spain, on March 11, 2004; the bombings in the London transportation system on July 7, 2005; and the bombing of a Red Sea resort at Sharm el-Sheikh in Egypt on July 23, 2005.

We are living in a dangerous, confused, and troubled world that demands leaders, educators, and classroom teachers who can bridge cultural, ethnic, and religious borders, envision new possibilities, invent novel paradigms, and engage in personal transformation and visionary action. The concepts, paradigms, and projects that facilitated the rise and triumph of the West between the 16th and the 20th centuries are ineffective in the recreated world of the 21st century.

The world is undergoing a transformation—and in the words of Thomas L. Friedman (2005)—"the world is flat." In the flat world described by Friedman, scientific and technological workers educated in Asian nations such as India and China are competing successfully with—and sometimes outperforming—scientific and technological workers educated at universities in the United States, the United Kingdom, and other Western nations. The Western nations can no longer take their scientific and technological superiority for granted because of the leap in scientific and technological education in Asian nations such as India and China.

Balancing Unity and Diversity

Multicultural societies are faced with the problem of constructing nation-states that reflect and incorporate the diversity of their citizens and yet have an overarching set of shared values, ideals, and goals to which all of their citizens are committed (Banks, 1997). Only when a nation-state is unified around a set of democratic values such as justice and equality can it protect the rights of cultural, ethnic, language, and religious groups and enable them to experience cultural democracy and freedom. Kymlicka (1995), a Canadian political theorist, and Rosaldo (1997), a New York University anthropologist, have constructed theories about diversity and citizenship. Both Kymlicka and Rosaldo argue that in a democratic society, ethnic and immigrant groups should have the right to maintain their cultures and languages as well as to participate in the national civic culture. Kymlicka calls this concept "multicultural citizenship"; Rosaldo refers to it as "cultural citizenship." In 1920, Drachsler called it "cultural democracy."

Cultural, ethnic, racial, language, and religious diversity exists in most nations around the world. One of the challenges for diverse democratic nation-states is to provide opportunities for various groups to maintain aspects of their community cultures while building a nation in which these groups are structurally included and to which they feel allegiance. *A delicate balance of diversity and unity should be an essential goal of democratic nation-states and of teaching and learning in democratic societies* (Banks et al., 2001). Unity must be an important aim when nation-states are responding to diversity within their populations. They can protect the rights of minorities and enable diverse groups to participate only when they are unified around a set of democratic values such as justice and equality (Gutmann, 2004).

Citizenship education must be transformed in the 21st century because of the deepening racial, ethnic, cultural, language, and religious diversity in nation-states around the world. Citizens in a diverse democratic society should be able to maintain attachments to their cultural communities as well as participate effectively in the shared national culture. *Unity without diversity results in cultural repression and hegemony. Diversity without unity leads to Balkanization and the fracturing of the nation-state.* Diversity and unity should coexist in a delicate balance in democratic multicultural nation-states.

Nations such as France, the United Kingdom, The Netherlands, Australia, and Japan are struggling to balance unity and diversity. France prevented Muslin girls from wearing a headscarf to state schools because it is a religious symbol. This was an attempt to deal with the issue of unity and diversity within the context of the French concept of integration, which interprets equality to mean that "citizens . . . should be treated *identically* under the law . . . [and] that no distinction can be made between citizens on the basis of race, religion or national origin" (Limage, 2000, pp. 74–75). The riots in France in 2005 indicated that the French notion of integration is not functioning effectively in the real world (Geary & Graff, 2005). Many Arab and Muslim youths are alienated in France; they have a difficult time attaining a French identity and believe that most White French citizens do not view them as French. On November 7, 2005, a group of young Arab males in France were interviewed on the public television station (PBS) in the United States. One of the young men said, "I have French papers but when I go to the police station they treat me like I am not French." The French prefer the term *integration* to *race relations* or *diversity,* and *integration* has been officially adopted by the state. Integration is predicated on the assumption that differences are or should be reduced during the process of integration (Hargreaves, 1995).

The London subway and bus bombings that killed at least 56 people and injured more than 700 on July 7, 2005, deepened ethnic and religious tension and Islamophobia in Europe after the police revealed that the suspected perpetrators were Muslim suicide bombers. The young men who were accused of these bombings were British citizens who apparently had weak identities with most of their fellow White mainstream British citizens.

Defining Citizenship and Citizenship Education

The definition of *citizen* in *Webster's Encyclopedic Unabridged Dictionary of the English Language* (1989, p. 270) is a "native or naturalized member of a state or nation who owes allegiance to its government and is entitled to its protection." This same dictionary defines *citizenship* as the "state of being vested with the rights, privileges, and duties of a citizen" (p. 270). Absent from these minimal definitions of *citizen* and *citizenship* are the deep and complex meanings of these terms in democratic multicultural societies that were developed by the scholars who participated in a conference on diversity and citizenship education held in Bellagio, Italy, in 2002 that was sponsored by the Center for Multicultural Education at the University of Washington (Banks, 2004a).

The scholars at the Bellagio conference stated that citizens within democratic multicultural nation-states endorse the overarching ideals of the nation-state such as justice and equality, are committed to the maintenance and perpetuation of these ideals, and are willing and able to take action to help close the gap between their nation's democratic ideals and practices that violate those ideals, such as social, racial, cultural, and economic inequality (Banks, 2004a). Consequently, an important goal of citizenship education in a democratic multicultural society is to help students acquire the knowledge, attitudes, and skills needed to make reflective decisions and to take actions to make their nation-states more democratic and just (Banks, 1997).

To become thoughtful decision makers and citizen actors, students need to master social science knowledge, clarify their moral commitments, identify alternative courses of action, and act in ways consistent with democratic values (Banks, 2006c; Banks & Banks, with Clegg, 1999). Gutmann (2004) states that democratic multicultural societies are characterized by *civic equality, toleration,* and *recognition.* Consequently, an important goal of citizenship education in multicultural societies is to teach toleration and recognition of cultural differences. Gutmann views *deliberation* as an essential component of democratic education in multicultural societies. Gonçalves e Silva (2004), a Brazilian scholar, states that citizens in a democratic society work for the betterment of the whole society, not just for the rights of their particular racial, social, or cultural group. She writes:

> A citizen is a person who works against injustice not for individual recognition or personal advantage, but for the benefit of all people. In realizing this task—shattering privileges, ensuring information and competence, acting in favor of all—each person becomes a citizen. (p. 197)

Gonçalves e Silva (2004) also states that becoming a citizen is a *process* and that education must play an important role to facilitate the development of *civic consciousness* and *agency* within students. She provides powerful examples of how civic consciousness and agency are developed in community schools for the children of Indigenous peoples and Blacks in Brazil. Osler (2005) points out that students should experience citizenship within the schools and should not be "citizens-in-waiting."

Multiple Views of Citizenship

In the discussion of his citizenship identity in Japan, Murphy-Shigematsu (2004) describes how complex and contextual citizenship identification is within a multicultural nation-state such as Japan. Becoming a legal citizen of a nation-state does not necessarily mean that an individual will attain structural inclusion into the mainstream society and its institutions or will be perceived as a citizen by most members of the dominant group within the nation-state. *A citizen's racial, cultural, language, and religious characteristics often significantly influence whether she is viewed as a citizen within her society.* It is not unusual for American citizens to assume that Asian Americans born in the United States emigrated from another nation. Asian Americans are sometimes asked, "What country are you from?"

Brodkin (1998) makes a conceptual distinction between *ethnoracial assignment* and *ethnoracial identity* that is helpful in considering the relationship between citizenship identification and citizenship education. She defines ethnoracial assignment as the way outsiders define people within another group. Ethnoracial identities are how individuals define themselves "within the context of ethnoracial assignment" (p. 3). Individuals who are Arab Americans, citizens of the United States, and have a strong national identity as Americans are sometimes defined by many of their fellow American citizens as non-Americans (Gregorian, 2003).

The Bellagio Diversity and Citizenship Education Project

Citizenship education needs to be changed in significant ways because of the increasing diversity within nation-states throughout the world and the quests by racial, ethnic, cultural, and religious groups for cultural recognition and rights (Banks, 2004a; Castles, 2004). The Center for Multicultural Education at the University of Washington has implemented a project to reform citizenship education so that it will advance democracy as well as be responsive to the needs of cultural, racial, ethnic, religious, and immigrant groups within multicultural nation-states.

The first part of this project consisted of a conference, "Ethnic Diversity and Citizenship Education in Multicultural Nation-States," held at the Rockefeller Foundation's Study and Conference Center in Bellagio, Italy, June 17–21, 2002. The conference, which was supported by the Spencer and Rockefeller Foundations, included participants from 12 nations: Brazil, Canada, China, Germany, India, Israel, Japan, Palestine, Russia, South Africa, the United Kingdom, and the United States.

The papers from this conference are published in a book titled *Diversity and Citizenship Education: Global Perspectives* (Banks, 2004a). One of the conclusions of the Bellagio conference was that world migration and the political and economic aspects of globalization are challenging nation-states and national borders (Banks, 2004a). At the same time, national borders remain tenacious; the number of nations in the world is increasing rather than decreasing. The number of U.N. member states increased from 80 in 1950 to 191 in 2002 (Castles, 2004). Globalization and nationalism are coexisting and sometimes conflicting trends and forces in the world today (Banks et al., 2005). Consequently, educators throughout the world should rethink and redesign citizenship education courses and programs. Citizenship education should help students acquire the knowledge, attitudes, and skills needed to function in their nation-states as well as in a diverse world society that is experiencing rapid globalization and quests by ethnic, cultural, language, and religious groups for recognition and inclusion. Citizenship education should also help students to develop a commitment to act to change the world to make it more just.

Another conclusion of the Bellagio Conference is that citizenship and citizenship education are defined and implemented differently in various nations and in different social, economic, and political contexts (Banks, 2004a). Citizenship and citizenship education are contested ideas in nation-states around the world. However, there are shared problems, concepts, and issues, such as the need to prepare students in various nations to function within as well as across cultural and national borders.

The conference also concluded that these shared issues and problems should be identified by an international group that would formulate guidelines for dealing with them.

Democracy and Diversity

In response to the Bellagio Conference recommendations, the Center for Multicultural Education at the University of Washington created an International Consensus Panel that was supported by the Spencer Foundation in Chicago and the University of Washington. The Consensus Panel formulated four principles and identified 10 concepts for educating citizens for democracy and diversity in a global age. The Panel's report is titled *Democracy and Diversity: Principles and Concepts for Educating Citizens in a Global Age* (Banks et al., 2005). Its principles and concepts are in Table 2.1. The entire report can be downloaded as a pdf file at http://depts. washington.edu/centerme/DemDiv.pdf.

One of the conclusions of *Democracy and Diversity* is that diversity describes the wide range of racial, cultural, ethnic, linguistic, and religious variations that exists within and across groups that live in multicultural nation-states. The publication presents a broad view of diversity and points out that the variables of diversity—such as race, gender, social class, and religion—interact in complex ways and are highly interactive and interrelated. Consequently, a student might be female, Mexican American, Catholic, and working class at the same time. Each of these group memberships will influence her behavior. However, how these variables influence her behavior will vary with the specific context and situation. For example, her ethnic group may influence her behavior more significantly when she is at home and in her community than when she is at school. The dynamic relationships of the variables of diversity are illustrated in Figure 2.1.

Assimilationist Theory and Citizenship Education

In the assimilationist conception of citizenship education that existed in the United States and in other Western nations prior to the Civil Rights movement of the 1960s and 1970s, community cultures and languages of students from diverse groups were to be eradicated. One consequence of assimilationist citizenship education was that many students lost their first cultures, languages, and ethnic identities (Wong Fillmore, 2005). Some students also became alienated from their families and communi-

TABLE 2.1   **Principles and Concepts for Educating Citizens in a Global Age**

Principles
Section I. Diversity, Unity, Global Interconnectedness, and Human Rights

1. Students should learn about the complex relationships between unity and diversity in their local communities, the nation, and the world.
2. Students should learn about the ways in which people in their community, nation, and region are increasingly interdependent with other people around the world and are connected to the economic, political, cultural, environmental, and technological changes taking place across the planet.
3. The teaching of human rights should underpin citizenship education courses and programs in multicultural nation-states.

Section II. Experience and Participation

4. Students should be taught knowledge about democracy and democratic institutions, and they should be provided opportunities to practice democracy.

Concepts

1. Democracy
2. Diversity
3. Globalization
4. Sustainable Development
5. Empire, Imperialism, Power
6. Prejudice, Discrimination, Racism
7. Migration
8. Identity/Diversity
9. Multiple Perspectives
10. Patriotism and Cosmopolitanism

Source: J. A. Banks et al. (2005), *Democracy and Diversity: Principles and Concepts for Educating Citizens in a Global Age.* Seattle: University of Washington, Center for Multicultural Education. Reprinted with permission.

ties. Another consequence was that many students became socially and politically alienated within the national civic culture, as many Muslim youths in France and the United Kingdom are today (Modood, Triandafyllidou, & Zapata-Barrero, 2006).

Members of identifiable racial groups often become marginalized in both their community cultures and in the national civic culture because they can function effectively in neither. When they acquire the language and culture of the mainstream dominant culture, they are often denied structural inclusion and full participation into the civic culture because

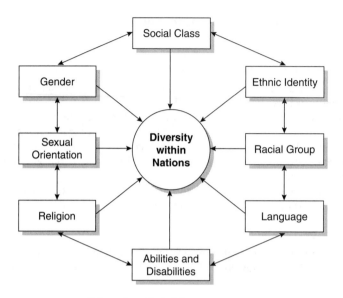

FIGURE 2.1   Diversity Variables

Source: Adapted from J. A. Banks (2001), *Cultural Diversity and Education: Foundations, Curriculum, and Teaching* (4th ed.). Boston: Allyn and Bacon, p. 76. Copyright © 2007 by James A. Banks. Reprinted with author's permission.

of their racial characteristics (Alba & Nee, 2003; Gordon, 1964). Teachers and schools must practice democracy and human rights in order for these ideals to be internalized by students. The concept of democracy conceptualized in this book includes *cultural democracy* in addition to political and economic democracy. Cultural democracy means that students have a right to express their cultural identity and to use their home languages in schools.

Schools and classrooms must become microcosms and exemplars of democracy and social justice in order for students to develop democratic attitudes and learn how to practice democracy. As Dewey (1959) stated, "All genuine education comes through experience" (p. 13). However, much work must be done—in nation-states throughout the world—before most teachers and schools in democratic multicultural nation-states actualize democracy and social justice in their curricula, teaching materials, and in their attitudes, expectations, and behaviors.

Multicultural democratic nation-states must find ways to help students develop balanced and thoughtful attachments and identifications with their cultural community, their nation-state, and the global community. In some cases, such as in the European Union and in parts of

Asia, it is also important for citizens to develop a regional identification. Nation-states have generally failed to help students develop a delicate balance of identifications. Rather, they have given priority to national identifications and have neglected the community cultures of students as well as the knowledge and skills students need to function in an interdependent global world.

Nationalists and assimilationists—in nation-states throughout the world—worry that if they help students develop identifications and attachments to their cultural communities, they will not acquire sufficiently strong attachments to their nation-states. Kymlicka (2004) points out that nationalists have a "zero-sum conception of identity" (p. xiv). Nussbaum (2002) believes that a focus on nationalism may prevent students from developing a commitment to cosmopolitan values such as human rights and social justice—values that transcend national boundaries, cultures, and times. Nussbaum states that we should help students develop *cosmopolitanism.*

Cosmopolitanism and Local Identity

Cosmopolitans view themselves as citizens of the world. Nussbaum states that their "allegiance is to the worldwide community of human beings" (p. 4)." She contrasts cosmopolitan universalism and internationalism with parochial ethnocentrism and inward-looking patriotism. She points out, however, that "to be a citizen of the world one does not need to give up local identifications, which can be a source of great richness in life" (p. 4).

Appiah (2006), another proponent of cosmopolitanism, also views local identities as important. He writes:

> In the final message my father left for me and my sisters, he wrote, "Remember you are citizens of the world." But as a leader of the independence movement in what was then the Gold Coast, he never saw a conflict between local partialities and universal morality—between being a part of the place you were and a part of a broader human community. . . .
> Raised with this father and an English mother, who was both deeply connected to our family in England and fully rooted in Ghana, where she has now lived for half a century, I always had a sense of family and tribe that was multiple and overlapping; nothing could have seemed more commonplace. (p. xviii)

Identity is multiple, changing, overlapping, and contextual, rather than fixed and static. The multicultural conception of identity is that citizens who have clarified and thoughtful attachments to their community cultures, languages, and values are more likely than citizens who are stripped of their cultural attachments to develop reflective identifications with their nation-state (Banks, 2004b; Kymlicka, 2004). They will also be better able to function as effective citizens in the global community. Nation-states, however, must make structural changes that reduce structural inequality and that legitimize and give voice to the hopes, dreams, and visions of their marginalized citizens in order for them to develop strong and clarified commitments to the nation-state and its goals.

The Development of Cultural, National, Regional, and Global Identifications

Assimilationist notions of citizenship are ineffective today because of the deepening diversity throughout the world and the quests by marginalized groups for cultural recognition and rights. *Multicultural citizenship* is essential for today's global age (Kymlicka, 1995). It recognizes and legitimizes the right and need of citizens to maintain commitments both to their cultural communities and to the national civic culture. Only when the national civic culture is transformed in ways that reflect and give voice to the diverse ethnic, racial, language, and religious communities that constitute it will it be viewed as legitimate by all of its citizens (Banks, 2004b; Kymlicka, 1995). Only then can they develop clarified commitments to the nation-state and its ideals.

Students should develop a delicate balance of cultural, national, regional, and global identifications and allegiances. (See Figure 2.2.) Citizenship education should help students to develop thoughtful and clarified identifications with their cultural communities and their nation-states (Banks, 2004b). Regional identifications are especially important for students who live in some parts of the world, such as in the European Union (Osler, 2000) and in Asia (Lee et al., 2004). Citizenship education should also help students to develop clarified global identifications and deep understandings of their roles in the world community. Students need to understand how life in their cultural communities and nations influences other nations and the cogent influence that international events have on their daily lives. Global education should have as major goals helping students to develop understandings of the interdependence among nations in the world today, clarified attitudes toward other nations, and reflective identifications with the world community. I conceptualize global identification similar to the way in which Nussbaum (2002) and Appiah (2006) define *cosmopolitanism*.

Nonreflective and unexamined cultural attachments may prevent the development of a cohesive nation with clearly defined national goals and policies (Banks, 2004b). Although we need to help students

FIGURE 2.2   **Cultural, National, Regional, and Global Identifications**

Source: Adapted from J. A. Banks, Ed. (2004), *Diversity and Citizenship Education: Global Perspectives.* San Francisco: Jossey-Bass. Reprinted with permission.

develop reflective and clarified cultural identifications, they must also be helped to clarify their identifications with their nation-states. However, blind nationalism may prevent students from developing reflective and positive regional and global identifications. Nationalism and national attachments in most nations are strong and tenacious. An important aim of citizenship education should be to help students develop global identifications. Students also need to develop a deep understanding of the need to take action as citizens of the global community to help solve the world's difficult global problems. Cultural, national, regional, and global experiences and identifications are interactive and interrelated in a dynamic way (Banks, 2004b). (See Figure 2.2.)

A nation-state that alienates and does not structurally include all cultural groups into the national culture runs the risk of creating alienation and causing groups to focus on their specific concerns and issues rather than on the overarching goals and policies of the nation-state. To develop reflective cultural, national, regional, and global identifications, students must acquire the knowledge, attitudes, and skills needed to function within and across diverse groups and the commitment to make their nations and the world more just and humane.

Dimensions and School Characteristics

One problem that continues to haunt the multicultural education movement—from both within and without—is the tendency by the public, teachers, administrators, and policy makers to oversimplify the concept. Multicultural education is complex and multidimensional, yet media commentators and educators alike often focus on only one of its many dimensions. Some teachers view it only as the inclusion of content about ethnic groups into the curriculum; others view it as prejudice reduction; still others view it as the celebration of ethnic holidays and events. Some educators view it as a movement to close the achievement gap between White mainstream students and low-income students of color. After a presentation in a school in which I described the major goals of multicultural education, a math teacher told me that what I said was fine and appropriate for language arts and social studies teachers but it had nothing to do with mathematics teachers like him. After all, he said, math was math, regardless of the color of the students.

The Dimensions of Multicultural Education

This statement by a respected teacher at a prestigious independent school, and his reaction to multicultural education, caused me to think deeply about the images of multicultural education that had been created by the key theorists in the field. I wondered whether we were partly responsible for this teacher's narrow conception of multicultural education as merely content integration. It was in response to these kinds of statements by classroom teachers that I conceptualized the dimensions of multicultural education. I use the dimensions in this chapter to describe the field's major components and to highlight important developments within the last two decades (Banks, 2004a). The dimensions of multicultural education are (1) content integration, (2) the knowledge construction process, (3) prejudice reduction, (4) an equity pedagogy, and (5) an empowering school culture and social structure. (See Figure 3.1.)

Content Integration

Content integration deals with the extent to which teachers use examples, data, and information from a variety of cultures and groups to illustrate the key concepts, principles, generalizations, and theories in their subject area or discipline. In many school districts as well as in popular writings, multicultural education is viewed only (or primarily) as content integration. This narrow conception of multicultural education is a major reason that many teachers in subjects such as biology, physics, and mathematics believe that multicultural education is irrelevant to them and their students.

In fact, this dimension of multicultural education probably does have more relevance to social studies and language arts teachers than it does to physics and math teachers. Physics and math teachers can insert multicultural content into their subjects, for example, by using biographies of physicists and mathematicians of color and examples from different cultural groups. However, these kinds of activities are probably not the most important multicultural tasks that can be undertaken by science and math teachers. Activities related to the other dimensions of multicultural education—such as the knowledge construction process, prejudice reduction, and an equity pedagogy—are probably the most fruitful areas for the multicultural involvement of science and math teachers.

The Knowledge Construction Process

The knowledge construction process describes the procedures by which social, behavioral, and natural scientists create knowledge and how the implicit cultural assumptions, frames of reference, perspectives, and biases within a discipline influence the ways that knowledge is constructed within it. The knowledge construction process is an important part of multicultural teaching. Teachers help students to understand how knowledge is created and how it is influenced by the racial, ethnic, gender, and social-class positions of individuals and groups.

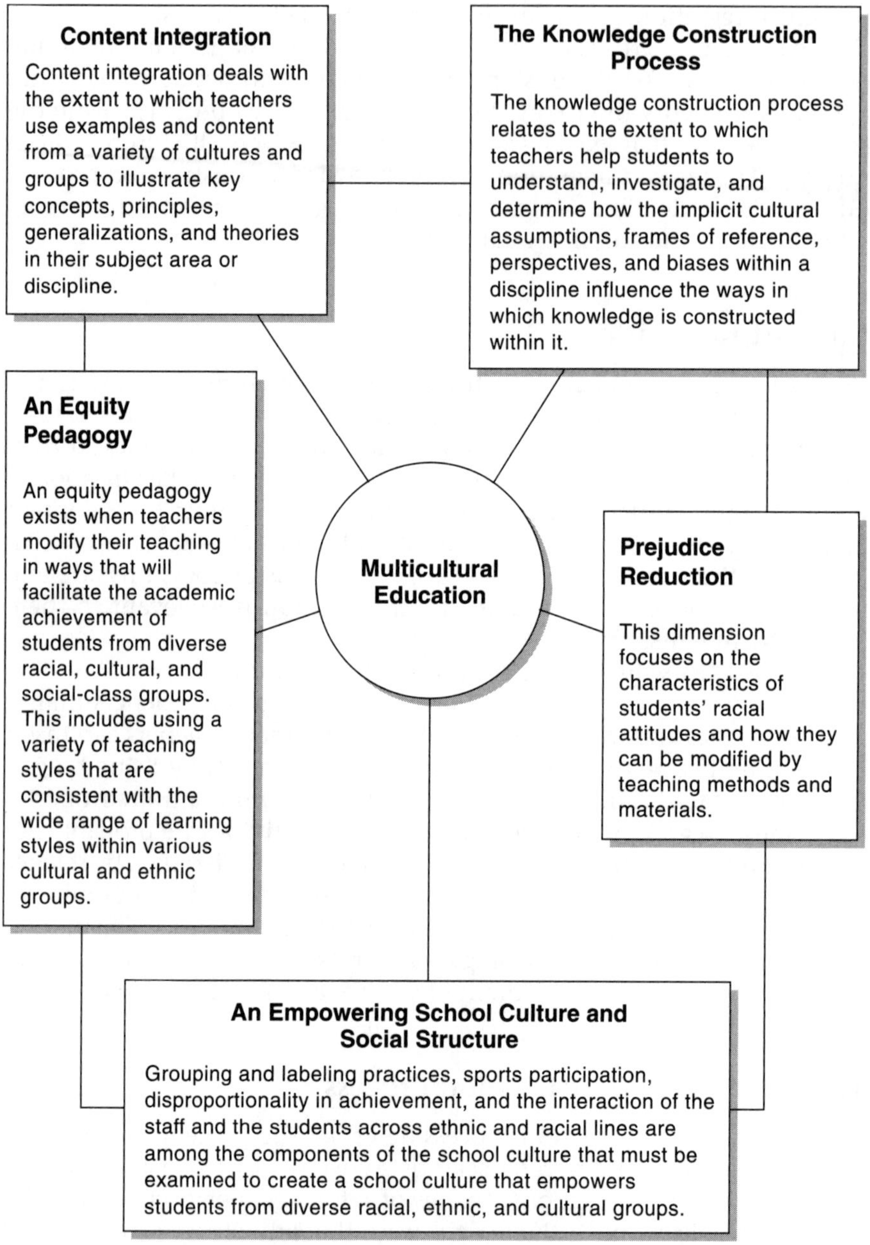

Content Integration

Content integration deals with the extent to which teachers use examples and content from a variety of cultures and groups to illustrate key concepts, principles, generalizations, and theories in their subject area or discipline.

The Knowledge Construction Process

The knowledge construction process relates to the extent to which teachers help students to understand, investigate, and determine how the implicit cultural assumptions, frames of reference, perspectives, and biases within a discipline influence the ways in which knowledge is constructed within it.

An Equity Pedagogy

An equity pedagogy exists when teachers modify their teaching in ways that will facilitate the academic achievement of students from diverse racial, cultural, and social-class groups. This includes using a variety of teaching styles that are consistent with the wide range of learning styles within various cultural and ethnic groups.

Multicultural Education

Prejudice Reduction

This dimension focuses on the characteristics of students' racial attitudes and how they can be modified by teaching methods and materials.

An Empowering School Culture and Social Structure

Grouping and labeling practices, sports participation, disproportionality in achievement, and the interaction of the staff and the students across ethnic and racial lines are among the components of the school culture that must be examined to create a school culture that empowers students from diverse racial, ethnic, and cultural groups.

FIGURE 3.1   The Dimensions of Multicultural Education

Source: J. A. Banks (2006), *Cultural Diversity and Education: Foundations, Curriculum, and Teaching* (5th ed.). Boston: Allyn and Bacon, p. 5. Reprinted with permission.

Important landmark work related to the construction of knowledge has been done by feminist social scientists and epistemologists as well as by scholars in ethnic studies. Working in philosophy and sociology, Sandra Harding (1991, 1998), Lorraine Code (1991), and Patricia Hill Collins (2000) have done some of the most important work in knowledge construction. This seminal work, although influential among scholars and curriculum developers, has been overshadowed in the popular media by the polarized canon debates. These writers and researchers have seriously challenged the claims made by the positivists that knowledge is value free and have described the ways in which knowledge claims are influenced by the gender and ethnic characteristics of the knower. These scholars argue that the human interests and value assumptions of those who create knowledge should be identified, discussed, and examined.

Code (1991) states that the gender of the knower is epistemologically significant, because knowledge is both subjective and objective, and that both aspects should be recognized and discussed. Collins (2000), an African American sociologist, extends and enriches the works of writers such as Code (1991) and Harding (1991) by describing the ways in which race and gender interact to influence knowledge construction. Collins calls the perspective of African American women "the outsider-within perspective." She writes, "As outsiders within, Black women have a distinct view of the contradictions between the dominant group's actions and ideologies" (p. 11).

Curriculum theorists, scholars in multicultural education, and historians are conceptualizing and developing ways to apply the work being done by the feminist and ethnic studies epistemologists to the classroom. My book *Teaching Strategies for Ethnic Studies* (Banks, 2003) contains conceptual and transformative lessons for teaching about the various ethnic groups, including African Americans, Mexican Americans, Asian Americans, and European Americans. Rethinking Schools, Ltd., a nonprofit educational publisher in Milwaukee founded by teachers, publishes a number of publications that help teachers conceptualize and teach transformative lessons about diversity, including *Rethinking Our Classrooms: Teaching for Equity and Justice*, Volume 2 (Bigelow et al., 2001) and *Rethinking Globalization: Teaching for Justice in an Unjust World* (Bigelow & Peterson, 2002). Loewen has written three books that contain transformative perspectives about race in the United States that are highly accessible and useful for teachers: *Lies My Teachers Told Me: Everything Your American History Textbook Got Wrong* (Loewen, 1995); *Lies Across America: What Our Historic Sites Get Wrong* (Loewen, 1999); and *Sundown Towns: A Hidden Dimension of American Racism* (Loewen, 2005).

Prejudice Reduction

The prejudice reduction dimension of multicultural education describes the characteristics of children's racial attitudes and strategies that can be used to help students to develop more positive racial and ethnic attitudes (Stephan & Vogt, 2004; Stephan, 1999). Since the 1960s, social scientists have learned a great deal about how racial attitudes in children develop and about ways in which educators can design interventions to help children to acquire more positive feelings toward other racial groups. I have reviewed that research in two other publications (Banks, 2002; 2006a), and readers are referred to them for a comprehensive discussion of this topic. Stephan and Vogt (2004), Stephan (1999), and Stephan and Stephan (2004) also provide extensive discussions of the research on children's racial attitudes and strategies that can be used to help students attain democratic racial attitudes and behaviors.

This research tells us that by the age of four, African American, White, and Mexican American children are aware of racial differences and often make racial preferences that are biased toward Whites. Students can be helped to develop more positive racial attitudes if realistic images of ethnic and racial groups are included in teaching materials in a consistent, natural, and integrated fashion. Involving students in vicarious experiences and in cooperative learning activities with students of other racial groups will also help them to develop more positive racial attitudes and behaviors. Researchers such as Cross (1991) and Wright (1998) question the research that shows that African American children have negative attitudes toward themselves and other African Americans. Chapter 7 of this book includes a comprehensive discussion of the racial attitudes of students and ways to help them develop more positive racial attitudes and behaviors.

Equity Pedagogy

An equity pedagogy exists when teachers use techniques and teaching methods that facilitate the academic achievement of students from diverse racial, ethnic, and social-class groups. Using teaching techniques that are responsive to the learning and cultural characteristics of diverse groups (Au, 2006; González, Moll, & Amanti, 2005; Mahiri, 2004), and using cooperative learning techniques (Cohen & Lotan, 1997), are some of the teaching techniques teachers have found effective with students from diverse racial, ethnic, social-class, and language groups.

If teachers are to increase learning opportunities for all students, they must be knowledgeable about the social and cultural contexts of teaching and learning (Au, 2006; Lee, 2007). Although students are not solely products of their cultures and vary in the degree to which they identify with them, there are some distinctive cultural behaviors associated with ethnic groups (Au, 1979; Boykin, 2000). Effective teachers are aware of the distinctive backgrounds of their students and have the skills to translate that knowledge into effective instruction (Gay, 2000).

Research indicates that teachers can increase the classroom participation and academic achievement of students from different cultural and language groups by modifying their instruction so that it draws upon their cultural strengths. Some studies provide evidence to support the idea that when teachers use culturally responsive teaching, the academic achievement of students from diverse groups increases. Au and Kawakami (1985) found that when teachers used participation structures in lessons that were similar to the Hawaiian speech event "talk story," the reading achievement of Native Hawaiian students increased significantly. They write:

> The chief characteristic of talk story is *joint performance*, or the cooperative production of responses of two or more speakers. For example, if the subject is going surfing, one of the boys begins by recounting the events of a particular day. But he will immediately invite one of the other boys to join him in describing the events to the group. The two boys will alternate as speakers, each telling a part of the story, with other children present occasionally chiming in. (Au & Kawakami, 1985, p. 409) (emphasis in original)

Talk story is very different from recitations in most classrooms, in which the teacher usually calls on an individual child to tell a story.

Lee (2007) found that the achievement of African American students increases when they are taught literary interpretations with lessons that use the African American verbal practice of *signifying*. Signifying is "a genre within African American English speech that involves ritual insult—as in playing the dozens. Signifying always involves . . . [a] high use of figurative language" (Carol Lee, e-mail communication, February 5, 2005).

An Empowering School Culture and Social Structure

An empowering school culture and social structure describes the process of restructuring the culture and organization of the school so that students from diverse racial, ethnic, language, and social-class groups will experience educational equality and empowerment. This dimension of multicultural education involves conceptualizing the school as a unit of change and making structural changes within the school environment so that students from all groups will have an equal opportunity for success. Establishing assessment techniques that are fair to all groups (Kornhaber, 2004; Pellegrino, Chudowsky, & Glaser, 2001), detracking the school (Oaks, 2005), and creating the norm among the school staff

TABLE 3.1   The Eight Characteristics of the Multicultural School

1. The teachers and school administrators have high expectations for all students and positive attitudes toward them. They also respond to them in positive and caring ways.

2. The formalized curriculum reflects the experiences, cultures, and perspectives of a range of cultural and ethnic groups as well as of both genders.

3. The teaching styles used by the teachers match the learning, cultural, and motivational characteristics of the students.

4. The teachers and administrators show respect for the students' first languages and dialects.

5. The instructional materials used in the school show events, situations, and concepts from the perspectives of a range of cultural, ethnic, and racial groups.

6. The assessment and testing procedures used in the school are culturally sensitive and result in students of color being represented proportionately in classes for the gifted and talented.

7. The school culture and the hidden curriculum reflect cultural and ethnic diversity.

8. The school counselors have high expectations for students from different racial, ethnic, and language groups and help these students to set and realize positive career goals.

that all students can learn—regardless of their racial, ethnic, or social-class groups—are important goals for schools that wish to create a school culture and social structure that is empowering and enhancing for students from diverse groups.

Characteristics of a Multicultural School

To implement the dimensions of multicultural education, schools and other educational institutions must be reformed so that students from all social-class, racial, cultural, and language groups and from both gender groups will have an equal opportunity to learn and experience cultural empowerment (Banks & Banks, 2007). Educational institutions should also help all students to develop more democratic values, beliefs, and actions and the knowledge, skills, and attitudes needed to function cross-culturally.

What parts of the school need to be reformed in order to implement the dimensions of multicultural education? A reformed school that exemplifies the dimensions has the eight characteristics listed in Table 3.1. Consequently, school reform should be targeted on the following school variables:

1. Attitudes, perceptions, beliefs, and actions of the school staff. Research indicates that teachers and administrators often have low expectations for language minority students, low-income students, and students of color (Gay, 2000; Green, 2000). In a restructured multicultural school, teachers and administrators have high academic expectations for all students and believe that all students can learn (Brookover et al., 1979; Edmonds, 1986; Ladson-Billings, 1994).

2. Formalized curriculum and course of study. The curriculum in most schools shows most concepts, events, and situations from the perspectives of mainstream Americans (Banks, 2003). It often marginalizes the experiences of people of color and of women. Multicultural education reforms the curriculum so that students view events, concepts, issues, and problems from the perspectives of diverse racial, ethnic, language, and social-class groups (Banks, 2006b; Takaki, 1993). The perspectives of both men and women are also important in the restructured, multicultural curriculum.

3. Learning, teaching, and cultural characteristics favored by the school. Research indicates that a large number of low-income, linguistic minority, Latino, Native American, and African American students have learning, cultural, and motivational characteristics that differ from the teaching styles that are used most frequently in the schools (Au, 2006; Lee, 2007; Stipek, 2004). These students often learn best when cooperative rather than competitive teaching techniques are used (Cohen & Lotan, 1997). Many of them also learn best when school rules and learning outcomes are made explicit and expectations are made clear (Delpit, 1995).

4. Languages and dialects of the school. Many students come to school speaking languages and dialects of English that differ from the standard English being taught. Although all students must learn standard English in order to function successfully in the wider society, the school should respect the first languages and varieties of English that students speak (Gracía, 2005). Many African American students come to school speaking what many linguists call Ebonics, or "Black English" (Alim & Baugh, 2007; Smitherman, 2000). In the restructured, multicultural school, teachers and administrators respect the languages and dialects of English that students come to school speaking and use the students' first languages and dialects as vehicles for helping them to learn standard English (Stritikus & Varghese, 2007).

5. Instructional materials. Many biases—sometimes latent—are found in textbooks and other instructional materials. These materials often marginalize the experiences of people of color, language minorities, women, and low-income people and focus on the perspectives of men who are members of the mainstream society. In the restructured, multicultural school, instructional materials are reformed and depict events from diverse ethnic and cultural perspectives (Banks, 2003). Teachers and students are also taught to identify and challenge the biases and assumptions of all materials.

6. Assessment and testing procedures. IQ and other mental ability tests often result in students of color, low-income students, and language minority students being overrepresented in classes for students with mental retardation and underrepresented in classes for students who are gifted and talented (Ford, 2007). Human talent, as well as mental retardation, is randomly distributed across human population groups. Consequently, in a restructured multicultural school, assessment techniques are used that enable students from diverse cultural, ethnic, and language groups to be assessed in culturally fair and just ways. In a restructured multicultural school, students of color and language minority students are found proportionately in classes for the gifted and talented (Ford, 2007). They are not heavily concentrated in classes for mentally retarded students (Artiles & Zamora-Duran, 1997).

7. The school culture and the hidden curriculum. The hidden curriculum has been defined as the curriculum that no teacher explicitly teaches but that all students learn. Jackson (1992) calls the hidden curriculum "untaught lessons." The school's attitudes toward cultural and ethnic diversity are reflected in many subtle ways in the school culture, such as the kinds of pictures on the bulletin boards, the racial composition of the school staff, and the fairness with which students from different racial, ethnic, cultural, and language groups are disciplined and suspended. Multicultural education reforms the total school environment so that the hidden curriculum sends the message that cultural and ethnic diversity is valued and celebrated.

8. The counseling program. In an effective multicultural school, counselors help students from diverse cultural, racial, ethnic, and language groups to make effective career choices and to take the courses needed to pursue those career choices (Sue, 2004). Culturally responsive counselors also help students to reach beyond their grasp, to dream, and to actualize their dreams.

Multicultural educators make the assumption that if the preceding eight variables within the school environment are reformed and restructured and the dimensions of multicultural education are implemented, students from diverse groups and of both genders will attain higher levels of academic achievement and the intergroup attitudes, beliefs, and behaviors of students from all groups will become more democratic.

4

Curriculum Transformation

It is important to distinguish between curriculum *infusion* and curriculum *transformation*. When the curriculum is infused with ethnic and gender content without curriculum transformation, the students view the experiences of cultural groups and of women from the perspectives and conceptual frameworks of the traditional Western canon (Bender, 2006; Levine, 1996). Consequently, groups such as Native Americans, Asian Americans, and Latinos are added to the curriculum, but their experiences are viewed from the perspective of mainstream historians and social scientists. When curriculum infusion occurs without transformation, women are added to the curriculum but are viewed from the perspectives of mainstream males. Concepts such as "The Westward Movement," "The European Discovery of America," and "Men and Their Families Went West" remain intact.

When curriculum transformation occurs, students and teachers make paradigm shifts and view the American and world experience from the perspectives of different racial, ethnic, cultural, and gender groups. Columbus's arrival in the Americas is no longer viewed as a "discovery" but as a cultural contact or encounter that had very different consequences for the Tainos (Arawaks), Europeans, and Africans (Hyatt & Nettleford, 1995). In a transformed curriculum, the experiences of women in the West are not viewed as an appendage to the experience of men but "through women's eyes" (Armitage, 1987; Limerick, 1987).

This chapter discusses the confusion over goals in multicultural education, describes its goals and challenges, and states the rationale for a transformative multicultural curriculum. Important goals of multicultural education are to help teachers and students transform their thinking about the nature and development of the United States and the world and also to develop a commitment to act in ways that will make the United States and the world more democratic and just.

The Meaning and Goals of Multicultural Education

A great deal of confusion exists—among both educators and the general public—about the meaning of multicultural education. The meaning of multicultural education among these groups varies from education about people in other lands to educating African American students about their heritage but teaching them little about the Western heritage of the United States. The confusion over the meaning of multicultural education is exemplified by a question the editor of a national education publication asked me: "What is the difference between multicultural education, ethnocentric education, and global education?" Later during a telephone interview, I realized that she had meant "Afrocentric education" rather than "ethnocentric education." To her, these terms were synonymous.

Before we can solve the problem caused by the multiple meanings of multicultural education, we need to better understand the causes of the problem. One important cause of the confusion over the meaning of multicultural education is the multiple meanings of the concept in the professional literature itself. Sleeter and Grant (1997), in their comprehensive survey of the literature on multicultural education, found that the term has diverse meanings and that about the only commonality the various definitions share is reform designed to improve schooling for students of color.

To advance the field and to reduce the multiple meanings of multicultural education, scholars need to develop a higher level of consensus about what the concept means. Agreement about the meaning of multicultural education is emerging among academics. A consensus is developing among scholars that an important goal of multicultural education is to increase educational equality for both gender groups, for students from diverse ethnic and cultural groups, and for exceptional students (Banks & Banks, 2007; Ladson-Billings & Gillborn, 2004). A major assumption of multicultural education is that some groups of students—because their cultural characteristics are more consistent with the culture, norms, and expectations of the school than are those of other groups of students—

have greater opportunities for academic success than do students whose cultures are less consistent with the school culture. Low-income African American males, for example, tend to have more problems in schools than do middle-class White males (Ferguson, 2001; Noguera, 2003b).

Because one of its goals is to increase educational equality for students from diverse groups, school restructuring is essential to make multicultural education become a reality. To restructure schools in order to provide all students with an equal chance to learn, some of the major assumptions, beliefs, and structures within schools must be radically changed. These include tracking and the ways in which mental ability tests are interpreted and used (Oakes, 2005; Kornhaber, 2004). New paradigms about the ways students learn, about human ability (Gardner, 2006; Gould, 1996), and about the nature of knowledge will have to be institutionalized in order to restructure schools and make multicultural education a reality. Teachers will have to believe that all students can learn, regardless of their social class or ethnic group membership, and that knowledge is a social construction that has social, political, and normative assumptions (Code, 1991; Collins, 2000). Implementing multicultural education within a school is a continuous process that cannot be implemented within a few weeks or over several years. The implementation of multicultural education requires a long-term commitment to school improvement and restructuring.

Another important goal of multicultural education—on which there is wide consensus among authorities in the field but that is neither understood nor appreciated by many teachers, journalists, and the public—is to help all students, including White mainstream students, to develop the knowledge, skills, and attitudes they will need to survive and function effectively in a future U.S. society in which about half the population will be people of color by 2050 (U.S. Census Bureau, 2000). Our survival as a strong and democratic nation will be seriously imperiled if we do not help our students attain the knowledge and skills they need to function in a culturally diverse future society and world. As Martin Luther King stated eloquently, "We will live together as brothers and sisters or die separate and apart as strangers" (King, 1987).

This goal of multicultural education is related to an important goal of global education—to help students to develop cross-cultural competency in cultures beyond our national boundaries and the insights and understandings needed to understand how all peoples living on the earth have highly interconnected fates (Banks et al., 2005). Citizens who have an understanding of and empathy for the cultures within their own nation are probably more likely to function effectively in cultures outside of their nation than are citizens who have little understanding of and empathy for cultures within their own society.

Although multicultural and global education share some important aims, in practice, global education can hinder teaching about ethnic and cultural diversity in the United States. Some teachers are more comfortable teaching about Mexico than they are teaching about Mexican Americans who live within their own cities and states. Other teachers, as well as some publishers, do not distinguish between multicultural and global education. Although the goals of multicultural and global education are complementary, they need to be distinguished both conceptually and in practice.

Multicultural Education Is for All Students

We need to think seriously about why multicultural educators have not been more successful in conveying to teachers, journalists, and the general public the idea that multicultural education is concerned not only with students of color and linguistically diverse students but also with White mainstream students. It is also not widely acknowledged that many of the reforms designed to increase the academic achievement of ethnic and linguistic minority students, such as a pedagogy that is sensitive to student learning characteristics and cooperative learning techniques, will also help White mainstream students to increase their academic achievement and to develop more positive intergroup attitudes and values (Cohen & Lotan, 1997; Gay, 2000).

It is important for multicultural education to be conceptualized as a strategy for all students for several important reasons. U.S. schools are not working as well as they should be to prepare all students to function in a highly technological, postindustrial society (Graham, 2005). Most students of color (with the important exception of some groups of Asian students such as Chinese Americans and Japanese Americans) and low-income students are more dependent on the school for academic achievement than are White middle-class students for a variety of complex reasons. However, school restructuring is needed for all students because of the high level of literacy and skills needed by citizens in a knowledge society and because of the high expectations that the public has for today's schools. Public expectations for the public schools have increased tremendously since the turn of the century, when many school leavers were able to get jobs in factories (Graham, 2005). School restructuring is an important and major aim of multicultural education.

Multicultural education should also be conceptualized as a strategy for all students because it will become institutionalized and supported in U.S. schools, colleges, and universities only to the extent that it is perceived as universal and in the broad public interest. An ethnic-specific notion of multicultural education stands little chance of success and implementation in the nation's educational institutions.

Challenges to the Mainstream Curriculum

Some readers might rightly claim that an ethnic-specific curriculum and education already exists in U.S. educational institutions and that it is Eurocentric and male dominated. I would agree to some extent with this claim. However, I believe that the days for the primacy and dominance of the mainstream curriculum are limited. The curriculum that is institutionalized within U.S. schools, colleges, and universities is being seriously challenged today and will continue to be challenged until it is reformed and more accurately reflects the experiences, voices, and struggles of people of color, of women, and of other cultural, language, and social-class groups in U.S. society. The curriculum within U.S. schools, colleges, and universities has changed substantially within the last three decades. It is important that these changes be recognized and acknowledged. Students in today's educational institutions are learning much more content about ethnic, cultural, racial, and gender diversity than they learned three decades ago. The ethnic studies and women's studies movements have had a significant influence on the curriculum in U.S. schools, colleges, and universities.

The dominance of the mainstream curriculum is much less complete and tenacious than it was before the Civil Rights and Women's Rights movements of the 1960s and 1970s. The historical, social, and economic factors are different today than they were when Anglo Americans established control over the major social, economic, and political institutions in the United States in the 17th and 18th centuries. The economic, demographic, and ideological factors that led to the establishment of Anglo hegemony early in U.S. history are changing, even though Anglo Americans are still politically, economically, and culturally dominant. Anglo dominance was indicated by the Supreme Court decisions that slowed the pace of affirmative action during the 1980s and that chipped away at civil rights laws protecting people with disabilities in 2001.

Nevertheless, there are signs throughout U.S. society that Anglo dominance and hegemony are being challenged and that groups such as African Americans, Asian Americans, and Latinos are increasingly demanding full structural inclusion and a reformulation of the canon used to select content for the school, college, and university curriculum (Hu-DeHart, 2004; West, 2004). It is also important to realize that many compassionate and informed Whites are joining people of color to support reforms in U.S. social, economic, political, and educational institutions. It would be a mistake to conceptualize or perceive the reform movements today as people of color versus Whites.

One pervasive myth within our society is that Whites are a monolithic group. The word *White* conceals more than it reveals. Whites are a very diverse group in terms of ethnic and cultural characteristics, political affiliations, and attitudes toward ethnic and cultural diversity (Howard, 2006). Many Whites today, as well as historically, have supported social movements to increase the rights of African Americans and other people of color (Branch, 2006). Reform-oriented White citizens who are pushing for a more equitable and just society are an important factor that will make it increasingly difficult for the Anglo mainstream vision to continue to dominate U.S. political and educational institutions.

Whites today are playing an important role in social reform movements and in the election of African American and Latino politicians (West, 2004). Many White students on university campuses are forming coalitions with students of color to demand that the university curriculum be reformed to include content about people of color and women. Students who are demanding ethnic studies requirements on university campuses have experienced major victories (Hu-DeHart, 2004).

The Anglocentric curriculum will continue to be challenged until it is reformed to include the voices and experiences of a range of ethnic, cultural, and language groups. Lesbian and gay groups are also demanding that content about them be integrated into the school, college, and university curriculum (Eisen & Hall, 1996; Lipkin, 1999). Colleges and universities are responding to the concerns of these groups much more effectively than are the schools.

The significant percentage of people of color, including African Americans and Latinos, who are in positions of leadership in educational institutions will continue to work to integrate the experiences of their people into the school and university curricula. These individuals include researchers, professors, administrators, and authors of textbooks. Students of color will continue to form coalitions with progressive White students and demand that the school and university curriculum be reformed to reflect the ethnic, cultural, and language reality of U.S. society. Students of color make up about 43 percent of the public school population in the United States today and are projected to make up 46 percent by 2020. Parents and community groups will continue to demand that the school and university curricula be reformed to give voice to their experiences and struggles. African American parents and community groups will continue to push for a curriculum that reflects African civilizations and experimental schools for Black males (Asante & Mazama, 2005).

Feminists will continue to challenge the mainstream curriculum because many of them view it as malecentric, patriarchal, and sexist. Much of the new research in women's studies deals with the cultures of women of color (Schmitz et al., 2004). Women's studies and ethnic studies will continue to interconnect and challenge the dominant curriculum in the nation's schools, colleges, and universities. Gay and lesbian groups will continue to demand that their voices, experiences, hopes, and dreams be reflected in a transformed curriculum (Eisen & Hall, 1996; Lipkin, 1999).

Challenges to Multicultural Education

I have argued that an ethnic-specific version of multicultural education is not likely to become institutionalized within U.S. schools, colleges, and universities and that the days of Anglo hegemony in the U.S. curriculum are limited. This is admittedly a long view of our society and future. Multicultural education is frequently challenged by conservative writers and groups (Huntington, 2004; Reich, 2002; Stotsky, 1999). These challenges are likely to continue, and will take diverse forms, expressions, and shapes. They are part of the dynamics of a democratic society in which diverse voices are freely expressed and heard.

I believe that part of the confused meanings of multicultural education results from the attempts by neoconservative scholars to portray multicultural education as a movement against Western civilization, as anti-White and, by implication, anti-American. The popular press frequently calls the movement to infuse an African perspective into the curriculum "Afrocentric," and it has defined the term to mean an education that excludes Whites and Western civilization.

The term *Afrocentric* has different meanings to different people. Because of its diverse interpretations by various people and groups, neoconservative scholars have focused many of their criticisms of multicultural education on this concept. Asante (1998) defines *Afrocentricity* as "placing African ideals at the center of any analysis that involves African culture and behavior" (p. 6). In other words, Afrocentricity is looking at African and African American behavior from an African or African American perspective. His definition suggests that Black English, or Ebonics, cannot be understood unless it is viewed from the perspective of those who speak it. Afrocentricity, when Asante's definition is used, can describe the addition of an African American perspective to the school and university curriculum. When understood in this way, it is consistent with a multicultural curriculum because a multicultural curriculum helps students to view behavior, concepts, and issues from different ethnic and cultural perspectives.

The Canon Battle: Special Interests
versus the Public Interest

The push by people of color and women to get their voices and experiences institutionalized within the curriculum and the curriculum canon transformed has evoked a strong reaction from some neoconservative scholars (Stotsky, 1999). Many of the arguments in the editorials and articles written by the opponents of multicultural education are smoke screens for a conservative political agenda designed not to promote the common good of the nation but to reinforce the status quo and dominant group hegemony and to promote the interests of a small elite. A clever tactic of the neoconservative scholars is to define their own interests as universal and in the public good and the interests of women and people of color as special interests that are particularistic (Ravitch, 1990). When a dominant elite describes its interests as the same as the public interests, it marginalizes the experiences of structurally excluded groups, such as women and people of color.

The term *special interest* implies an interest that is particularistic and inconsistent with the overarching goals and needs of the nation-state or commonwealth. To be in the public good, interests must extend beyond the needs of a unique or particular group. An important issue is who formulates the criteria for determining what is a special interest. It is the dominant group or groups in power that have already shaped the curriculum, institutions, and structures in their images and interests. The dominant group views its interests not as special but as identical with the common good. A special interest, in the view of those who control the curriculum and other institutions within society, is therefore any interest that challenges the dominant group's power and ideologies and paradigms, particularly if the interest group demands that the canon, assumptions, and values of the institutions and structures be transformed. History is replete with examples of dominant groups that defined their interests as the public interest.

One way in which people in power marginalize and disempower those who are structurally excluded from the mainstream is by calling their visions, histories, goals, and struggles special interests. This type of marginalization denies the legitimacy and validity of groups that are excluded from full participation in society and its institutions.

Only a curriculum that reflects the experiences of a wide range of groups in the United States and the world, and the interests of these groups, is in the national interest and is consistent with the public good. Any other kind of curriculum reflects a special interest and is inconsistent with the needs of a nation that must survive in a pluralistic and highly interdependent global world. Special interest history and literature, such as history and literature that emphasize the primacy of the West and the history of European American males, is detrimental to the public good because it will not help students to acquire the knowledge, skills, and attitudes essential for survival in the 21st century.

The aim of the ethnic studies and women's studies movements is not to push for special interests but to reform the curriculum so that it will be more truthful and more inclusive and will reflect the histories and experiences of the diverse groups and cultures that make up U.S. society. These are not special interest reform movements, because they contribute to the democratization of the school and university curriculum. They contribute to the public good instead of strengthening special interests.

We need to rethink concepts such as special interests, the national interest, and the public good and to identify which groups are using these terms and for what purposes and also to evaluate the use of these terms in the context of a nation and world that are rapidly changing. Powerless and excluded groups accurately perceive efforts to label their visions and experiences as special interests as an attempt to marginalize them and to make their voices silent and their faces invisible.

A Transformed Curriculum and Multiple Perspectives

Educators use several approaches, summarized in Figure 4.1, to integrate cultural content into the school and university curriculum (Banks, 2007). These approaches include the *contributions approach*, in which content about ethnic and cultural groups is limited primarily to holidays and celebrations, such as Cinco de Mayo, Asian/Pacific Heritage Week, African American History Month, and Women's History Week. This approach is used often in the primary and elementary grades. Another frequently used approach to integrate cultural content into the curriculum is the *additive approach*. In this approach, cultural content, concepts, and themes are added to the curriculum without changing its basic structure, purposes, and characteristics. The additive approach is often accomplished by the addition of a book, a unit, or a course to the curriculum without changing its framework.

Neither the contributions nor the additive approach challenges the basic structure or canon of the curriculum. Cultural celebrations, activities, and content are inserted into the curriculum within the existing curriculum framework and assumptions. When these approaches are used to integrate cultural content into the curriculum, people, events, and interpretations related to ethnic groups and women often reflect the

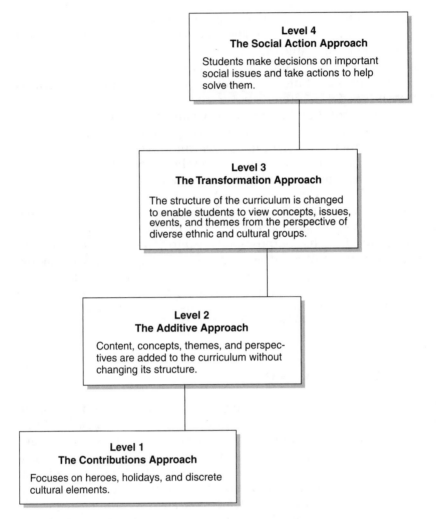

FIGURE 4.1   Approaches to Multicultural Curriculum Reform

norms and values of the dominant culture rather than those of cultural communities. Individuals and groups challenging the status quo and dominant institutions are less likely to be selected for inclusion in the curriculum. Thus, Sacajawea, who helped Whites conquer Native American lands, is more likely to be chosen for inclusion than Geronimo, who resisted the takeover of Native American lands by Whites.

The *transformation approach* differs fundamentally from the contributions and additive approaches. It changes the canon, paradigms, and basic assumptions of the curriculum and enables students to view concepts, issues, themes, and problems from different perspectives and points of view. Major goals of this approach include helping students to understand concepts, events, and people from diverse ethnic and cultural perspectives and to understand knowledge as a social construction. In this approach, students are able to read and listen to the voices of the victors and the vanquished. They are also helped to analyze the teacher's perspective on events and situations and are given the opportunity to formulate and justify their own versions of events and situations. Important aims of the transformation approach are to teach students to think critically and to develop the skills to formulate, document, and justify their conclusions and generalizations.

When teaching a unit such as "The Westward Movement" using a transformation approach, the teacher would assign appropriate readings and then ask the students such questions as: What do you think the Westward movement means? Who was moving West—the Whites or the Native Americans? What region in the United States was referred to as the West? Why? The aim of these questions is to help students to understand that the Westward movement is a Eurocentric term. It refers to the movement of the European Americans who were headed in the direction of the Pacific Ocean. The Lakota Sioux were already living in the West and, as Limerick (2000) insightfully points out, were trying hard to stay put. They did not want to move. The Sioux did not consider their homeland "the West" but the center of the universe. The teacher could also ask the students to describe the Westward movement from the point of view of the Sioux. The students might use such words as "The End," "The Age of Doom," or "The Coming of the People Who Took Our Land." The teacher could also ask the students to give the unit a name that is more neutral than "The Westward Movement." They might name the unit "The Meeting of Two Cultures."

The *decision-making and social action approach* extends the transformative curriculum by enabling students to pursue projects and activities that allow them to make decisions and to take personal, social, and civic actions related to the concepts, problems, and issues they have studied. After they have studied the unit on different perspectives on the Westward movement, the students might decide that they want to learn more about Native Americans and to take actions that will enable the school to depict and perpetuate more accurate and positive views of America's first inhabitants. The students might compile a list of books written by Native Americans for the school librarian to order and present a pageant for the school's morning exercise on "The Westward Movement: A View from the Other Side."

Teaching Students to Know, to Care, and to Act

Major goals of a transformative curriculum that fosters multicultural literacy should be to help students to know, to care, and to act in ways that will develop and foster a democratic and just society in which all groups experience cultural democracy and cultural empowerment. Knowledge is an essential part of multicultural literacy, but it is not sufficient. Knowledge alone will not help students to develop an empathetic, caring commitment to humane and democratic change. An essential goal of a multicultural curriculum is to help students develop empathy and caring. To help the United States and world become more culturally democratic, students must also develop a commitment to personal, social, and civic action as well as the knowledge and skills needed to participate in effective civic action.

Although knowledge, caring, and action are conceptually distinct, in the classroom they are highly interrelated. In my multicultural classes for teacher education students, I use historical and sociological knowledge about the experiences of different ethnic and racial groups to inform as well as to enable the students to examine and clarify their personal attitudes about ethnic diversity. These knowledge experiences are also a vehicle that enables the students to think of actions they can take to actualize their feelings and moral commitments. Knowledge experiences I have used to help students examine their value commitments and think of ways to act include the reading of *Balm in Gilead: Journey of a Healer*, Sara Lawrence Lightfoot's (1988) powerful biography of her mother, one of the nation's first African American child psychiatrists; the historical overviews of various U.S. ethnic groups in my book *Teaching Strategies for Ethnic Studies* (Banks, 2003); and several video and film presentations, including selected segments from *Eyes on the Prize II*, the award-winning history of the Civil Rights movement produced by Henry Hampton, and *Eye of the Beholder*, a powerful videotape that uses simulation to show the cogent effects of discrimination on adults. The videotape features Jane Elliott, who attained fame for her well-known experiment in which she discriminated against children on the basis of eye color to teach them about discrimination (Peters, 1987).

To enable the students to analyze and clarify their values regarding these readings and video experiences, I ask them questions such as: How did the book, film, or videotape make you feel? Why do you think you feel that way? To enable them to think about ways to act on their feelings, I ask such questions as: How interracial are your own personal experiences? Would you like to live a more interracial life? What are some books that you can read or popular films that you can see that will enable you to act on your commitment to live a more racially and ethnically integrated life? The power of these kinds of experiences is often revealed in student papers, as is illustrated by this excerpt from a paper written by a student after he had viewed several segments of *Eyes on the Prize II* (Muir, 1990):

> I feel that my teaching will now necessarily be a little bit different forever simply because I myself have changed. . . . I am no longer quite the same person I was before I viewed the presentations—my horizons are a little wider, perspectives a little broader, insights a little deeper. That is what I gained from *Eyes on the Prize*.

The most meaningful and effective way to prepare teachers to involve students in multicultural experiences that will enable students to know, to care, and to participate in democratic action is to involve teachers in multicultural experiences that focus on these goals. When teachers have gained knowledge about cultural and ethnic diversity themselves, looked at that knowledge from different ethnic and cultural perspectives, and taken action to make their own lives and communities more culturally sensitive and diverse, they will have the knowledge and skills needed to help transform the curriculum canon as well the hearts and minds of their students. Only when the curriculum canon is transformed to reflect cultural diversity will students in our schools, colleges, and universities be able to attain the knowledge, skills, and perspectives needed to participate effectively in today's global society.

Multicultural Education and National Survival

Multicultural education is needed to help all future citizens of the United States to acquire the knowledge, attitudes, and skills needed to survive in the 21st century. Nothing less than our national and global survival is at stake. The rapid growth in the nation's population of people of color; the escalating importance of non-White nations such as China, Japan, and India; and the widening gap between the rich and the poor make it essential for future citizens to have multicultural literacy and cross-cultural skills. A nation whose citizens cannot negotiate on the world's multicultural global stage are tremendously disadvantaged in the 21st century, and its very survival is imperiled.

5

Knowledge Components

Eight characteristics of the multicultural school are described in Chapter 3 (see Table 3.1, page 36). Each of these elements must be reformed in order to enable schools to create equal educational opportunities for all students and to help students develop the knowledge, skills, and attitudes needed to function effectively in a changing national and world society. One of the eight characteristics of an effective multicultural school identified in Table 3.1 is positive teacher attitudes and behaviors. To acquire the attitudes, perceptions, and behavior needed to actualize multicultural education in their schools, teachers need a sound knowledge base in multicultural education. This chapter describes the knowledge that teachers need to master in order to be effective in multicultural classrooms and schools.

The Four Knowledge Categories

To become effective multicultural teachers, teachers need the following:

1. Knowledge of the major paradigms in multicultural education
2. Knowledge of the major concepts in multicultural education
3. Historical and cultural knowledge of the major ethnic groups
4. Pedagogical knowledge about how to adapt curriculum and instruction to the unique needs of students from diverse cultural, ethnic, language, and social-class groups

This chapter focuses on the first three categories of knowledge. Chapter 6 describes pedagogical knowledge.

Multicultural Education Paradigms

A paradigm is an interrelated set of ideas that explain human behavior or a phenomenon. It implies policy and action and has specific goals, assumptions, and values. Paradigms compete with one another in the arena of ideas and public policy.

Since the 1960s, several major paradigms have been formulated explaining why many low-income students and students of color have low levels of academic achievement (Banks, 2006a; Banks & Banks, 2004). Two of these paradigms or explanations are the *cultural deprivation paradigm* and the *cultural difference paradigm*. These two paradigms have very different assumptions, research findings, and implications for teaching in multicultural classrooms. Teachers who embrace the cultural deprivation paradigm and those who embrace the cultural difference paradigm are likely to respond differently to low-income students and students of color in classroom interactions and to have different ideas about how to increase their academic achievement. See Banks (2006b) for a discussion of other paradigms.

The Cultural Deprivation Paradigm

Cultural deprivation theorists assume that low-income students do not achieve well in school because of the culture of poverty in which they are socialized. These theorists believe that characteristics such as poverty, disorganized families, and single-parent homes cause children from low-income communities to experience "cultural deprivation" and "irreversible cognitive deficits."

Cultural deprivationists assume that a major goal of the school is to provide "culturally deprived" students with cultural and other experiences that will compensate for their cognitive and intellectual deficits. These theorists believe that low-income students can learn the basic skills taught by the schools but that these skills must be taught using behaviorist methods and strategies.

Cultural deprivation theorists see the major problem as the culture of the students rather than the culture of the school. Teachers and administrators who embrace the cultural deprivation paradigm often blame the victims for their problems and academic failure (Rothstein, 2004). They assume that low-income students and students of color often do poorly in school because of their cultural and social-class characteristics, not because they are ineffectively taught. They believe that the school is limited in what it can do to help these students achieve because of the culture into which they are socialized. Advocates of this paradigm focus on changing the student rather than on changing the culture of the school to enable it to focus on the cultural strengths of students from diverse groups.

The Cultural Difference Paradigm

Unlike cultural deprivation theorists, cultural difference theorists reject the idea that low-income students and students of color have cultural deficits. They believe that ethnic groups such as African Americans, Mexican Americans, Asian Americans, and Native Americans have strong, rich, and diverse cultures (Gay, 2000; Alim & Baugh, 2007). These cultures consist of languages, values, behavioral styles, and perspectives that can enrich the lives of all Americans. Low-income students and students of color fail to achieve in school not because they have culturally deprived cultures but because their cultures are different from the culture of the school and the mainstream culture most valued by society (Ladson-Billings, 1994).

Cultural difference theorists believe that the school and inequality within the larger society—rather than the cultures of low-income students and students of color—are primarily responsible for the low academic achievement of low-income students and students of color (Au, 2006; Gonzáles, Moll, & Amani, 2005). The school must change in ways that will allow it to respect and reflect the cultures of low-income students and students of color and at the same time use teaching strategies that are consistent with their cultural characteristics. Culturally sensitive and enriched teaching strategies will motivate low-income students and students of color and will enable them to achieve at high levels (Boykin, 2000). The schools, argue cultural difference theorists, often fail to help low-income students and students of color to achieve because schools frequently ignore or try to alienate them from their cultures and rarely use teaching strategies that are consistent with their lifestyles. Cultural difference theorists frequently cite research that shows how the culture of the school and the cultures of low-income students and students of color differ in values, norms, and behaviors (Irvine, 2003; Ladson-Billings, 1994).

Much of the research developed by cultural difference theorists focuses on the language and learning characteristics of students of color. Linguists such as Alim and Baugh (2007) and Geneva Smitherman (2000) have described Black English, or Ebonics (the version of English spoken by many African Americans), as a rich version of English that is logical, consistent in style and usage, and very effective in communicating a sense of kinship and unity among African Americans. Many teachers, however, view Black English negatively. Sociolinguists urge teachers to view Black English from a positive perspective and to use it as a vehicle to help its speakers to learn standard English as an alternative dialect, not as a replacement for their first language (Delpit & Dowdy, 2002). Cultural difference theorists also advise teachers to view other languages spoken by their students, such as Spanish and Vietnamese, as strengths rather than as problems to be overcome (Stritikus & Varghese, 2007).

Research by cultural difference theorists such as Au (2006), Mahiri (2004), Gay (2000), and Ladson-Billings (1994) indicates that most African American, Hispanic, Native American, and Native Hawaiian students have some learning and cultural characteristics that are inconsistent with the school culture. This research indicates, for example, that Mexican American students tend to be more field sensitive than do mainstream White students. The learning and affective characteristics of field-sensitive and field-independent students differ in a number of significant ways (Ramirez & Castaneda, 1974). Field-sensitive students tend to like to work with others to achieve a common goal. They are more sensitive to the feelings and opinions of others than are field-independent students, who prefer to work independently and to compete and gain individual recognition.

Learning style theory is often misinterpreted and misused by teachers and other school practitioners (Irvine & York, 1995). It is often interpreted to mean that if a student is Latino or African American, she will have a field-sensitive learning style. This kind of thinking results in the formation of new stereotypes about students from diverse racial, ethnic, and language groups. Although some groups of African American and Latino students are more likely to have field-sensitive learning characteristics than are some groups of mainstream Anglo students, all kinds of learning styles are found among all groups of students. Educators should keep the complexity of group characteristics in mind when they read studies or theories about learning styles. Learning style theory is harmful when it is oversimplified by teachers and other school practitioners.

Concepts in Multicultural Education

Concepts are important ideas that scientists use to classify and categorize information, data, and ideas (see Chapter 6). The heart of a discipline or field of study is its key concepts, generalizations, and principles. Culture is a major concept in multicultural education. We now examine culture and two related concepts: *macroculture* and *microculture*.

Culture

There are many different definitions of *culture*, but there is no single definition that all social scientists would heartily accept. Culture can be defined as the way of life of a social group—the total human-made environment (Geertz, 1995; Levinson & Ember, 1996). Although culture is often defined in a way that includes all the material and nonmaterial aspects of group life, most social scientists today emphasize the intangible, symbolic, and ideational aspect of culture.

The values, symbols, interpretations, and perspectives are what distinguish one people from another in modernized societies, not artifacts, material objects, and other tangible aspects of human societies. Values, norms, and perspectives distinguish ethnic groups such as Native Americans, African Americans, and Jewish Americans rather than the foods they eat or the clothes they wear. The essence of an ethnic culture in a modernized society such as the United States is its unique values, beliefs, symbols, and perspectives. Consequently, when teachers teach about groups such as Native Americans and Mexican Americans by having the students build teepees or eat tacos, they have missed the essence of the cultures of these groups and given the students misleading and distorted conceptions of their cultures.

Cultures are dynamic, complex, and changing. When teaching about the cultures of groups such as African Americans, Jewish Americans, and Japanese Americans, the teacher should be careful to help students to understand how such factors as time of immigration, social class, region, religion, gender, exceptionality, and education influence the behaviors and values of both individuals and subgroups within an ethnic group. An East Coast, upper-middle-class, college-educated Chicana (Mexican American female) whose family has been in the United States since the early 1900s will differ in significant ways from a male Mexican migrant worker in California who has lived in the United States less than two decades.

Teachers should help students to understand the complex characteristics of ethnic groups in order to prevent students from developing new stereotypes when ethnic groups are studied in school. Any discussion of the general characteristics of an ethnic group must be mediated by a consideration of how individual members of the group may differ from the group norms and characteristics in significant ways. Table 5.1 describes some of the key variables on which individuals within an ethnic or cultural group may differ.

TABLE 5.1   **Variables within Ethnic Groups on Which Individuals Differ**

Variables	Understandings and Behavior	Levels of Competency
		1 2 3 4 5 6 7
Values and Behavioral Styles	The ability to understand and interpret values and behavioral styles that are normative within the ethnic group.	←——————→
	The ability to express values behaviorally that are normative within the ethnic group.	
	The ability to express behavioral styles and nuances that are normative within the ethnic group.	
Languages and Dialects	The ability to understand, interpret, and speak the dialects and/or languages within the ethnic culture.	←————————→
Nonverbal Communications	The ability to understand and accurately interpret the nonverbal communications within the ethnic group.	←————————→
	The ability to communicate accurately nonverbally within the ethnic group.	
Cultural Cognitiveness	The ability to perceive and recognize the unique components of one's ethnic group that distinguish it from other microcultural groups within the society and from the national macroculture.	←————————→
	The ability to take actions that indicate an awareness and knowledge of one's ethnic culture.	
Perspectives, Worldviews, and Frames of Reference	The ability to understand and interpret the perspectives, worldviews, and frames of reference normative within the ethnic group.	←————————→

(continued)

TABLE 5.1   Continued

Variables	Understandings and Behavior	Levels of Competency
	The ability to view events and situations from the perspectives, worldviews, and frames of reference normative within the ethnic group.	
Identification	The ability to have an identification with one's ethnic group that is subtle and/or unconscious.	←————————→
	The ability to take overt actions that show conscious identification with one's ethnic group.	

Source: James A. Banks (2006), *Cultural Diversity and Education: Foundations, Curriculum and Teaching* (5th ed.). Boston: Allyn and Bacon, p. 82. Reprinted with permission.

Macroculture and Microculture

The concept of culture as formulated by most social scientists does not deal with variations within the national culture or the smaller cultures within it. However, when dealing with multicultural education, it is necessary to describe variations within the national culture, because multicultural education focuses on equal educational opportunities for different groups within the national culture. Two related concepts can help us deal with cultural variation within the national culture. We can call the national or shared culture of the nation-state or society the big culture, or *macroculture*. The smaller cultures that constitute it can be called *microcultures*.

Every nation-state has overarching values, symbols, and ideations that are to some degree shared by all microcultures. Various microcultural groups within the nation, however, may mediate, interpret, reinterpret, perceive, and experience these overarching national values and ideals differently.

National, overarching ideals, symbols, and values can be described for various nation-states. Myrdal (1944), the Swedish economist, identifies values such as justice, equality, and human dignity as overarching values in the United States. He calls these the American creed values. Myrdal also describes the "American dilemma" as an integral part of U.S.

society. This dilemma results from the fact that even though most U.S. citizens internalize American creed values, such as justice and human dignity, they often violate them in their daily behavior. Myrdal concludes that a tremendous gap exists between American democratic ideals and American realities, such as racism and sexism. Other U.S. overarching values include the Protestant work ethic, an individualistic versus a group orientation, distance, and materialism and material progress.

Historical and Cultural Knowledge of Ethnic Groups

Teachers need a sound knowledge of the history and culture of ethnic groups in order to successfully integrate ethnic content into the school curriculum (Banks, 2003; Franklin & Moss, 2000; Gutierrez, 2004; Takaki, 1998; Painter, 2005). However, factual knowledge about ethnic groups is necessary but not sufficient. This knowledge needs to be organized and taught with key concepts (e.g., powerful ideas), themes, and issues in the experiences of ethnic and cultural groups. The experiences of ethnic groups in the United States can be viewed and compared using the eleven powerful key concepts and ideas summarized in Table 5.2. In the following subsections, I describe eleven key concepts and discuss how each can be used to view and study the experiences of selected ethnic groups. Chapter 6 contains teaching units that describe how to teach two of these concepts: *knowledge construction* and *revolution*.

TABLE 5.2   **Key Concepts to Guide the Study of Ethnic and Cultural Groups**

1. Origins and immigration
2. Shared culture, values, and symbols
3. Ethnic identity and sense of peoplehood
4. Perspectives, worldviews, and frames of reference
5. Ethnic institutions and self-determination
6. Demographic, social, political, and economic status
7. Prejudice, discrimination, and racism
8. Intraethnic diversity
9. Assimilation and acculturation
10. Revolution
11. Knowledge construction

Key Concepts for Studying the Experiences
of Ethnic and Cultural Groups

1. Origins and immigration. When studying about an ethnic group in the United States, it is important to examine its origins and immigration patterns. Most groups in the United States came from other lands. However, archeologists believe that Native Americans entered North America by crossing the Bering Strait between 40,000 and 45,000 years ago (Snipp, 2004). However, when studying about the origins of the first Americans, it is important to point out to students that many Native Americans believe that they were created in this land by the Great Spirit (Champagne, 1994). Both perspectives on the origins of Native Americans should be presented and respected in the multicultural classroom.

The ancestors of the Mexican Americans are also natives to the Americas. A new people were created when the Spanish *conquistadors* and the Indians of the Americas produced offspring, who were called *mestizos*. When the United States acquired about one-third of Mexico's territory at the end of the United States–Mexican War in 1848, about 80,000 Mexicans became U.S. citizens (Gonzales, 1999). Today, about half of the growth in the Mexican population results from immigration; the other half is from new births (U.S. Census Bureau, 2000).

2. Shared culture, values, and symbols. Most ethnic groups in the United States, especially ethnic groups of color, have unique cultures and values that resulted from an interaction of their original culture with the host culture in the United States, from ethnic institutions created partly as a response to discrimination, and from their social-class status. These cultures are still in the process of formation and change. Consequently, they are complex and dynamic. They cannot and should not be viewed as static.

Examples of unique values and cultures of ethnic groups include the strong family orientation of Italian Americans (McGoldrick, Giordano, & Pearce, 1996), the strong identity with their tribe and kinship group among Native Americans (Hirschfelder, 1995), and the group orientation of African Americans (White & Parham, 1990). Black English, a version of English spoken by many African Americans, is also an example of an ethnic cultural characteristic (Alim & Baugh, 2007; Smitherman, 2000).

3. Ethnic identity and sense of peoplehood. A shared sense of peoplehood and ethnic identity is one of the most important characteristics of ethnic groups in the United States (Alba, 1990). This shared sense of identity results from a common history and current experiences. Ethnic groups tend to view themselves and to be viewed by others as separate and apart from other groups in society and as "imagined communities" (Anderson,

1991). In the case of ethnic groups of color, such as African Americans and Mexican Americans, their shared sense of identity and peoplehood is reinforced by the racial discrimination they experience. The shared sense of identity of an ethnic group can and often does extend beyond national boundaries. The ethnic groups often view the members of their groups as a *diaspora* spread out into various parts of the world. Most Jews in New York and London share feelings about the Holocaust (Dershowitz, 1997; Jacoby, 2000). Most African Americans strongly identify with the struggle of the Blacks in South Africa and with Blacks in Brazil, which has the largest population of Blacks outside of Africa (Telles, 2004).

4. Perspectives, worldviews, and frames of reference. Members of the same ethnic group often view reality in a similar way and differently from other groups within a society. This results largely from their shared sense of peoplehood and identity previously described. Most Latinos in the United States tend to have positive views toward bilingual education and believe that their children should be able to speak both Spanish and English (Bhatia & Ritchie, 2004). However, because Latinos in the United States have diverse histories, origins, and social classes, there is a range of views on every issue within Latino communities, including bilingual education. Two noted Latinos who express conservative views on a range of issues, including bilingual education, are Richard Rodriguez (1982) and Linda Chavez (1991).

5. Ethnic institutions and self-determination. Many ethnic institutions were formed by groups in the United States in response to discrimination and segregation. Examples are African American churches (Battle, 2006); schools, colleges, and insurance companies; and Japanese and Jewish social organizations. Many of these institutions continue to exist today because they help ethnic groups to satisfy unique social, cultural, and educational needs. Other ethnic institutions—such as the National Association for the Advancement of Colored People, the Anti-Defamation League of B'nai B'rith, the League of United Latin-American Citizens, and the Japanese American Citizenship League—were formed to work for the civil rights of specific ethnic groups and to fight discrimination.

6. Demographic, social, political, and economic status. When acquiring knowledge about ethnic groups in the United States, their current demographic, social, political, and economic status need to be determined. The economic profile of Filipino Americans was one of the lowest in the United States in the 1960s. However, they now have a high economic status, primarily because of the large number of professional workers that immigrated to the United States from the Philippines during the 1970s and 1980s (Takaki, 1989). The population of Asians and Hispanics in the United States increased significantly between 2000 and 2004. Asians increased from 10.6 million to 12.3 million, a 16.4 percent increase. Pacific Islanders increased from 462,000 to 506,000, a 9.3 percent increase. Hispanics (of any race) increased by 17 percent, African Americans by 5 percent, and Whites by 3.5 percent. In 2004, the U.S. total population reached a record 293,655,400 (U.S. Census Bureau, 2006a).

The economic and educational status of an ethnic group can change. For example, there was significant improvement in the economic and educational status of African Americans and Hispanics during the 1960s and 1970s. However, during the 1980s these groups lost ground in both economic and educational status. Although they experienced gains during the 1990s, the poverty rates among African Americans and Hispanics are still significantly higher than among Whites. In 2000, the poverty rate for non-Hispanic Whites was 8.6 percent, compared to 24.7 percent for African Americans and 21.9 percent for Hispanics (U.S. Census Bureau, 2004).

7. Prejudice, discrimination, and racism. Whenever groups with different racial, ethnic, and cultural characteristics interact, ethnocentrism, discrimination, and racism develop (Lubiano, 1997; Roediger, 2005). When discrimination based on race becomes institutionalized within a society and the dominant group has the power to implement its racial ideology within these institutions, institutional racism exists. Groups such as African Americans, Native Americans, Asian Americans, and Latinos have been historically—and are today—victims of institutional racism in the United States. However, racism today is much more subtle and less blatant than it was prior to the Civil Rights movement of the 1960s and 1970s. Some of the most blatant forms were eradicated during that period, largely in response to the Civil Rights movement.

Prejudice, discrimination, and racism are important concepts for understanding the experiences of ethnic groups in the past, present, and future, not only in the United States but also in nations throughout the world (Back & Solomos, 2000; Solomos, 2003).

8. Intraethnic diversity. Even though ethnic groups share a culture, values, a sense of identity, and a common history, there are tremendous differences within ethnic groups. These important differences must always be kept in mind when we study an ethnic group (see Table 5.1). If not, we may create new stereotypes and misconceptions. These differences result from such factors as region (e.g., whether rural or urban), social class, religion, age, gender, sexual orientation, and political affiliation (see Figure 2.1 in Chapter 2, page 26). While it is important to recognize that ethnic groups share many important characteristics, keep in mind that we are describing groups, not individuals. An individual may embrace all or hardly any of the dominant characteristics of his or her ethnic group. This individual may also have a strong or a weak identity with his or her ethnic group.

9. Assimilation and acculturation. When an ethnic or cultural group assimilates, it gives up its characteristics and adopts those of another group (Alba & Nee, 2003; Portes & Rumbaut, 2001). Acculturation describes the process that occurs when the characteristics of a group are changed because of interaction with another cultural or ethnic group. When acculturation occurs, the interacting groups exchange cultural characteristics; thus, both are changed in the process.

Assimilation and acculturation are important for understanding the experiences of ethnic groups in the United States and the world. In most societies, the dominant ethnic or cultural group expects other groups to adopt its language, culture, values, and behavior. Moreover, the dominant group within a society is usually at least partially successful in getting other groups to adopt its culture and values because of the power that it exercises. Cultural conflict usually develops within modernized societies when ethnic minority groups hold on to many of their important cultural characteristics or when they are denied full participation in the dominant society after they have largely culturally assimilated. The dominant cultural group within a society, such as the Anglo-Saxon Protestants in the United States, often adopt cultural traits from ethnic groups of color, such as African Americans and Native Americans, without acknowledging them or giving them appropriate public recognition. The contributions that African Americans and Native Americans have made to American literature, government, and music are rarely acknowledged fully (Weatherford, 1991).

10. Revolution. A political revolution occurs when a fundamental change takes place in the leadership of a society (Brinton, 1962; Marshall, 1994), usually through violent upheaval and armed conflict. Other basic changes within a society, which often take place over a long period of time, are also described as revolutions, such as the industrial and agricultural revolutions. These latter revolutions are gradual transformations of a society rather than sudden changes. Revolution is an important concept for understanding the history of most ethnic groups in the United States because of the influence of revolutions on their past. Revolution is also an important concept in the history of ethnic groups in the United States because the ideas related to it—such as oppression, alienation, and hope for change—have been decisive in the history of U.S. ethnic groups as well as in the history of ethnic groups in other nations (Modood et al., 2006; Solomos, 2003).

In 1680, an important American revolution occurred when the Pueblo Indians in New Spain (New Mexico) rebelled against their Spanish conquerors. Though the revolution was not successful in the long run, because the Pueblos were eventually reconquered by the Spaniards with deadly vengeance, it is an important revolution in American history.

Students need to view a revolution from a multicultural perspective to fully understand it because it can have different meanings for different groups. For example, the American Revolution had different meanings for Anglo Loyalists, Anglo Revolutionaries, various Native American groups, and African Americans. Also, some ethnic groups fled to the United States in search of freedom after revolutions had occurred in their native lands. When Castro took control of Cuba in 1959, thousands of Cubans sought refuge in the United States. The Cuban refugees who came to the United States during and in the years following the Castro revolution constitute the bedrock of the Cuban American community (Olson & Olson, 1995).

11. Knowledge construction. When studying the history and contemporary experiences of ethnic and cultural groups in the United States, it is important for students to understand how knowledge and interpretations are constructed. They also need to understand how cultural experiences, biases, and values influence the knowledge construction process (Banks, 1996a). A transformative, multicultural curriculum also helps students to construct their own interpretations. The constructivist approach to teaching and learning is a key component of the transformative, multicultural curriculum.

When teachers engage students in knowledge construction, the students are given opportunities to participate in building knowledge and to construct their own interpretations of historical, social, and current events. The knowledge construction approach to teaching is constructivist in orientation and is influenced by the work of the Russian psychologist Lev S. Vygotsky (Lee & Smagorinsky, 2000).

Knowledge construction is influenced significantly by the group experience of the knower. The knowledge constructed within a group is incorporated into the group's legends, myths, heroes, and heroines, and it reflects the group's values and beliefs. For example, the Battle of Little Big Horn can be viewed as a noble defense of one's homeland (the Native American version) or as a vicious massacre of soldiers who were protecting Anglo American pioneers (the dominant Anglo American view at the time) (Garcia, 1993).

Knowledge construction is a powerful idea in multicultural education because it can be taught in all disciplines and content areas. It can be used to help students understand the values and assumptions that underlie the base-10 number system in mathematics, the scientific method in the natural and biological sciences, and literary interpretations in the language arts and humanities. Knowledge construction is also a powerful idea that can guide the development of activities and teaching strategies that will enable students to build their own interpretations of the past, present, and future.

C H A P T E R 6

Teaching with Powerful Ideas

Can you list all of the major battles that occurred during the American Revolution or name each of the 50 state capitals? If you are like most people, you can't. Research indicates that people forget a very large percentage of the facts they learn (Greeno, Collins, & Resnick, 1996). What most people remember about the American Revolution is not all of the major battles that occurred but the major reasons the revolution took place and what happened when it ended.

Most people can remember that many state capitals are located in smaller cities rather than in the largest city within a state. Albany, rather than New York City, is the capital of New York; Springfield is the capital of Illinois, not Chicago; Olympia is the capital of Washington, not Seattle.

People tend to remember big, powerful ideas rather than factual details. Big ideas are not only remembered longer, but they also help people gain a better understanding of events and phenomena, categorize and classify observations, and transfer knowledge from one situation to another.

The Conceptual Approach

The big, powerful ideas that people tend to remember and that facilitate understanding and transfer of knowledge are called *concepts* and *generalizations* (Banks & Banks, 1999). In the conceptual approach to teaching, the curriculum as well as units and lessons are organized around key

65

concepts and generalizations from the various disciplines and subject areas. These powerful ideas help students to organize and synthesize large amounts of data and information (Taba et al., 1971) and to understand the fundamental ideas of disciplines and school subjects, which Bruner called "structure" in his classic book *The Process of Education*, first published in 1960.

The Categories of Knowledge

In order to develop and teach a multicultural curriculum that focuses on powerful concepts and ideas, you need to understand the knowledge categories and their interrelationships: facts, concepts, and generalizations. *Facts* are low-level, specific empirical statements. *Concepts* are words or phrases that enable people to categorize or classify a large class of observations and thus to reduce the complexity of their world. *Generalizations* are tested or verified statements that contain two or more concepts and state how they are related. Table 6.1 contains examples of facts, concepts, and generalizations.

Generalizations in this book are very similar to what Wiggins and McTighe (1998) call "big ideas." Generalizations are big ideas that contain powerful concepts. Wiggins and McTighe maintain that *understanding* requires that students explore, question, play with, and use big ideas in realistic contexts. Understanding also requires them to rephrase big

TABLE 6.1   **The Categories of Knowledge**

Concept: *Social Protest*

Fact: On February 1, 1960, the sit-in movement designed to end racially segregated accommodation facilities began when a group of African American students sat down at a lunch counter reserved for Whites at a Woolworth's store in Greensboro, North Carolina.

Lower-Level Generalization: The sit-in movement, boycotts, and the Black Power movement were part of a larger movement in the 1960s and 1970s whose goal was to end institutionalized racism and discrimination.

Intermediate-Level Generalization: The Civil Rights movement in the United States spread as women, people with disabilities, and gays and lesbians started organized movements to end discrimination against their respective groups.

High-Level/Universal Generalization: When a group perceives itself as oppressed and believes that there is a possibility for a change and reform, it will initiate organized protest and resistance.

ideas and verify them as important. Here are several examples of what Wiggins and McTighe call big ideas:

> Two light beams intersecting at crest and trough can cancel each other out and cause darkness.
>
> Correlation is not causation. Modern science, economics, and medicine deal more with the former than the latter.
>
> Negative and imaginary numbers are no less and no more real than ordinary numbers. They exist to provide symmetry and continuity needed for essential arithmetic and algebraic laws. (p. 113)

The discussion of concepts and generalizations is succinct and brief in this book. Readers who would like a more detailed discussion of knowledge categories as well as historical overviews of the major U.S. ethnic groups are referred to *Teaching Strategies for Ethnic Studies* (Banks, 2003).

A Conceptual Multicultural Curriculum

To build a conceptual, multicultural curriculum, it is necessary to choose higher-level powerful concepts such as *culture, power, socialization, protest*, and *values* as organizing concepts. One of the best conceptual curricula was developed by Hilda Taba and her colleagues (Taba et al., 1971). It is a social studies curriculum designed for grades 1 through 8. The Taba Social Studies Curriculum is organized around these powerful organizing concepts: causality, conflict, cooperation, cultural change, differences, interdependence, modification, power, societal control, tradition, and values.

Powerful organizing concepts for an interdisciplinary multicultural curriculum may be discipline specific, such as *culture* from anthropology and *socialization* from sociology. They may also be interdisciplinary, such as *modification* and *causality*, used in the Taba Social Studies Curriculum.

How to Develop a Multicultural Conceptual Curriculum

1. Identify key concepts, such as *ethnic diversity, immigration*, and *assimilation*, around which you will organize your curriculum. When choosing concepts around which to organize your curriculum, lessons, or units, keep the following criteria in mind:

a. The concepts should be powerful ones that can be used to organize a large quantity and scope of data and information.

b. The concepts should be ones that can be used to organize and classify information from a range of disciplines and subject areas, such as the social sciences, literature and the language arts, and, when possible, the physical, natural, and biological sciences. *Ethnic diversity* is such a concept (see Table 6.2).

c. Consider the developmental level of your students, in terms of their chronological age, cognitive development, moral development, and their prior experiences with ethnic and cultural content. Prejudice and discrimination are much more appropriate concepts to teach young children than is racism.

Taba and her colleagues (1971, p. 28) recommend that the first four questions guide the selection of key concepts for a conceptual curriculum. I have added the fifth question.

(1) Validity: Do they adequately represent the concepts of the disciplines from which they are drawn?

(2) Significance: Can they explain important segments of the world today, and are they descriptive of important aspects of human behavior?

(3) Durability: Are they of lasting importance?

(4) Balance: Do they permit development of student thinking in both scope and depth?

(5) Ethnic and cultural relevance: Do they help students to better understand the experiences of ethnic groups in the United States and around the world?

2. Identify key or universal generalizations related to each of the key concepts chosen.

3. Identify an intermediate-level generalization for each of the key concepts.

4. Identify a lower-level generalization related to the key generalization for each of the subject areas in which the key concept will be taught. The multicultural conceptual curriculum is *interdisciplinary*. Concepts are selected that can be used to incorporate information and data from several disciplines. In the example in Table 6.2, *ethnic diversity* is taught in each subject area. In actual practice, the concepts are likely to be taught in only two or three subject areas at the same time. Interdisciplinary teaching often requires team planning and teaching at the middle school level and beyond. Table 6.2 shows *ethnic diversity* being taught in each subject area to illustrate the powerful potential of the conceptual approach to teaching.

5. Formulate teaching strategies and activities to teach the concepts and generalizations. Teaching strategies for the following concepts are described in the second part of this chapter: (a) the construction of historical knowledge and (b) revolutions.

TABLE 6.2   **Teaching Ethnic Diversity in All Subject Areas**

Key Concept: *Ethnic diversity*

Key or Organizing Generalization: Most societies are characterized by ethnic diversity.

Intermediate-Level Generalization: Ethnic diversity is an important characteristic of the United States.

Lower-Level Generalizations:

Social Studies
The new wave of immigration to the United States since the 1960s has increased ethnic diversity within it.

Language Arts
Ethnic diversity is reflected in the variety of language and communication patterns in the United States.

Music
Ethnic diversity in the United States is reflected in its folk, gospel, and popular music.

Drama
The plays written by U.S. authors of varying ethnic backgrounds have enriched the national culture.

Physical and Movement Education
Dance and other forms of expressive movements in the United States reflect the nation's ethnic diversity.

Art
The visual arts in the United States reflect the nation's rich ethnic makeup.

Home Economics and Family Living
Ethnic diversity in the United States is reflected in the nation's foods and family lifestyles.

Science
The diverse physical characteristics of the people in the United States reinforce ethnic diversity.

Mathematics
Mathematical notations and systems in the United States reflect the contributions of many different ethnic, racial, and cultural groups. This is rarely recognized.

The Spiral Development of Concepts and Generalizations

In a conceptual, multicultural curriculum, the key concepts and generalizations identified are taught and developed at an increasing degree of complexity and depth throughout the grades. New content samples are used at each subsequent grade level to help students learn the concepts and generalizations at an increasing degree of depth and complexity. Figure 6.1 illustrates how *social protest*, a concept, is introduced in grade 5 and is taught with increasing depth and complexity through grade 12.

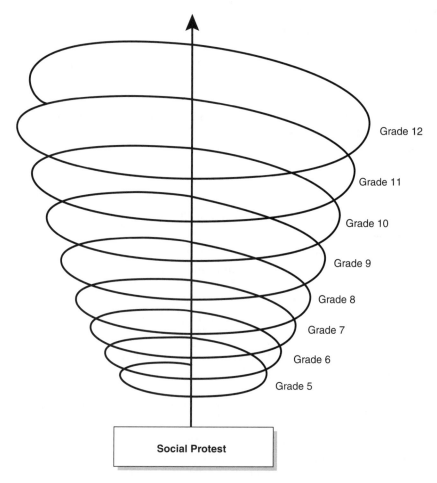

FIGURE 6.1   Social Protest Is Taught at Grades 5 through 12 at an Increasing Degree of Depth and Complexity

Social Science and Value Inquiry Skills

It is very important for students to master facts, concepts, and generalizations, but it is just as important, if not more so, for them to gain proficiency in the processes involved in gathering and evaluating knowledge, identifying the biases and assumptions that underlie knowledge claims,

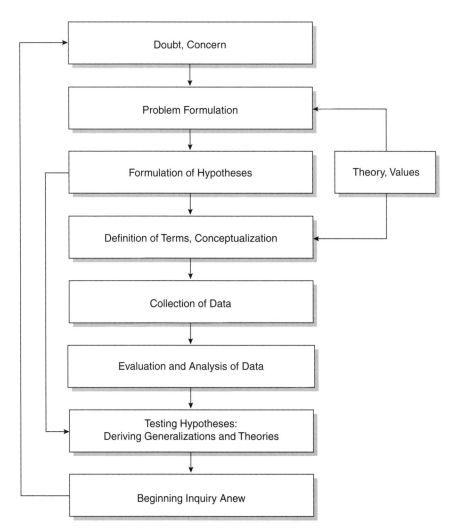

FIGURE 6.2 Model of Social Inquiry

Source: J. A. Banks & C. A. McGee Banks, with A. A. Clegg, Jr. (1999), *Teaching Strategies for the Social Studies: Decision-Making and Citizen Action* (5th ed.). New York: Longman, p. 68. Reprinted with permission.

and constructing knowledge themselves. An important goal of the multicultural curriculum is to help students develop proficiency in inquiry and thinking skills, such as stating research questions and problems, hypothesizing, conceptualizing, collecting and analyzing data, and deriving generalizations and conclusions.

The steps of social science inquiry, following a model developed by Banks (Banks & Banks, with Clegg, 1999), are illustrated in Figure 6.2. Note that in the inquiry model, doubt and concern cause the inquirer to formulate a problem. The problem that she formulates does not emanate from a vacuum, but is shaped by her theoretical and value orientation. Like the social scientist, the student will need to draw on *knowledge* to be able to ask intelligent and fruitful questions. In social science inquiry, *theory* is the main source of fruitful questions. While these are the basic steps of social inquiry, they do not necessarily occur in the order illustrated above. Figure 6.2 indicates that generalizations in social science are continually tested and are never regarded as absolute. Thus, social inquiry is cyclic rather than linear and fixed.

Although knowledge and skills goals are very important, it is essential that a multicultural curriculum help students develop the skills needed to reflect on their moral choices and to make thoughtful decisions. I have developed a value inquiry model (described on pages 87–88) that can be used to help students develop value inquiry skills. Students should be provided with opportunities to develop democratic values and to act on their moral decisions. Values education is especially important in multicultural education because prejudice and discrimination, which multicultural education tries to reduce, are heavily value laden. The moral dimension of multicultural education is discussed in the last part of this chapter.

Examples of Lessons Organized with Powerful Concepts

Teaching about Historical Bias and Knowledge Construction

The knowledge construction component of multicultural education helps students understand how knowledge is constructed and how it is influenced by the biases, experiences, and perceptions of historians and other researchers (Code, 1991; Collins, 2000; Harding, 1991). It also helps students to construct their own versions of the past, present, and future. In knowledge construction lessons and units, students are active participants in building knowledge rather than passive consumers of the knowledge constructed by others. What follows is a unit written by the author (Banks, with Sebesta, 1982) that is designed to teach junior high students how knowledge is constructed in history and about how historical interpretations are derived.

Columbus and the Arawaks

During the 15th century, Europeans wanted to find an easy way to reach Asia. They wanted to trade with Asian merchants. Many Europeans knew that the world is round. They believed they could reach Asia by sailing west. Christopher Columbus, an Italian sailor and explorer, was one person who wanted to prove that it could be done. For many years, he tried to find money to sail west to reach Asia, also called the East Indies. Finally, King Ferdinand and Queen Isabella of Spain agreed to support his voyage. On August 3, 1492, Columbus sailed from Palos, Spain. His three small ships were called the *Pinta,* the *Niña,* and the *Santa Maria.* On October 12, 1492, Columbus and his crew landed on San Salvador in the Bahama Islands. The Bahama Islands are located in what are now called the West Indies. We use that name because of the mistake Columbus made. He was sure he had landed near India. Even after other European explorers visited America, people still believed that America was part of the East Indies. This is why the Europeans called the Native Americans "Indians."

Columbus Writes about the Arawaks
In a letter that Columbus wrote in 1493, he tells of meeting with the people he called Indians (Muzzey, 1915, p. 8).

> They believed very firmly that I, with these ships and crews, came from the sky. . . . Wherever I arrived they went running from house to house and to the neighboring villages, with loud cries of "Come! Come to see the people from Heaven!"

Columbus Describes the Arawaks at San Salvador
Columbus kept a diary of his first voyage across the ocean. Here is what he wrote about the Arawaks when he first met them on San Salvador (Jane, 1989, pp. 23–24). Does he report facts only? Does he mix his own opinion with the facts?

> In fact, they took all and gave all, such as they had, with good will, but it seemed to me that they were a people very deficient in everything. They all go naked as their mothers bore them, and the women also, although I saw only one very young girl. And all those whom I did see were youths, so that I did not see one who was over thirty years of age; they were very well built, with very handsome bodies and very good faces. Their hair is coarse almost like the hairs of a horse's tail and short; they wear their hair down over their eyebrows,

except for a few strands behind, which they wear long and never cut. Some of them are painted black, and they are the colour of the people of the Canaries, neither black nor white, and some of them are painted white and some red and some in any colour that they find. Some of them paint their faces, some their whole bodies, some only the eyes, and some only the nose. They do not bear arms or know them, for I showed to them swords and they took them by the blade and cut themselves through ignorance.

They should be good servants and of quick intelligence, since I see that they very soon say all that is said to them, and I believe that they would easily be made Christians, for it appeared to me that they had no creed. Our Lord willing, at the time of my departure I will bring back six of them to Your Highnesses, that they may learn to talk. I saw no beast of any kind in this island, except parrots.

The Second Voyage of Columbus

Columbus sailed back to Spain on January 16, 1493. Later that same year, he set off on his second voyage. This time he explored other islands, including those now called Puerto Rico, the Virgin Islands, and Jamaica.

On his first trip, Columbus had established a trading post on the island of Hispaniola, where Haiti and the Dominican Republic are now located. When he returned to Hispaniola, he found that his trading post had been destroyed. This is what had happened. The men Columbus had left in charge of the trading post had been cruel to the Arawaks. The Arawaks became angry. One of them was a man named Caonabo (ka o na' bo). He led a group of Arawaks who killed the Spaniards and then destroyed the trading post. When Columbus discovered what had happened, he and his men attacked the Arawaks and defeated them. Caonabo was sent to Spain for punishment.

Columbus's Demands for Gold

Columbus set up a new trading post right away. It was very important for him to find gold in America and send it back to Spain. He had to please the Spanish king and queen.

Columbus did not really have any way of knowing how much gold there was in Hispaniola. In order to get as much gold as possible, he devised a plan. He told the Arawaks in the region yielding the gold that they must honor the Spanish king. Every three months, all of the Arawaks 14 years old or older had to give Columbus a small amount of gold dust. Each Arawak who gave the gold wore a piece of brass or copper around his or her neck to prove that the payment had been made. Any Arawak found without the neck ornament was punished. There was not enough gold in Hispaniola to satisfy Columbus. The Arawaks could not meet his demand for gold. Some tried to escape to the mountains. Some became ill and died. Some starved. Some who could not pay the gold were tortured and killed. Others were forced to work the land or were sent in slavery to Spain.

The Arawaks

What was life really like for the Arawaks? Their culture came to an end a century after the Spaniards came to their home in the Caribbean Islands.

But archaeologists, using artifacts, are able to piece together the story of the Arawaks.

An archaeologist named Fred Olsen (1974) studied Arawak artifacts. From what he learned from these artifacts, he wrote a description of what an Arawak community was probably like. He tried to tell what life was like for the Arawaks in 1490, which was two years before Columbus came to San Salvador in the Bahama Islands. Here is Fred Olsen's description of what might have happened during one day in an Arawak village:

> Along the edge of the river men are mending fishing nets. Others are collecting a shrub which contains a fish poison. One man is pounding the roots and stems until they are in shreds like hemp. Some of this mass is thrown into a large pool near the shore of the river. In a matter of minutes fish begin to rise and float on the surface. Young boys wade in, gleefully picking up the fish and bringing them ashore.
>
> At the end of the village pottery is being made by the women. At one spot a brush heap is slowly burning out and the pots lying on the embers are almost fully fired. A few more branches are put on the fire to finish baking the pots.
>
> Nearby two women are kneading the reddish plastic mass they have brought from the valley where good potter's clay is found not far from the river. Small amounts of water and sand are being added until the clay has the desired consistency. Experienced hands roll long rods of clay, about the thickness of a finger, which they coil layer by layer until the basic pot shape is formed. Smooth disks of stone, which they have picked up on the beach, are held snugly in the palm of the hand and the coils rubbed down until the ridges disappear and the bowl takes on a satinlike surface on both the outside and inside walls. (p. 218)

When Columbus first came to the Caribbean Islands in 1492, there were about three hundred thousand Arawaks living there. One hundred years later, almost none remained. Forced labor and diseases destroyed most of the Arawaks.

The Last Journeys of Columbus

Columbus made his two final journeys in 1498 and 1502. During these voyages, he sailed along the coast of Central America and South America. Columbus died in 1506, still thinking he had reached the Indies. He never knew that he had explored the continent of America.

In this unit, you have read about the landing of Columbus in America, and the effect he and other Spaniards had on the Arawaks. In the next chapter, you will read about other European explorers who came to America.

What Do You Think?

1. Columbus wrote in his diary that he thought the Indians had no religious beliefs. You read about Arawak life in the report by Fred Olsen. Do you think Columbus was correct? Why?
2. Accounts written by people who took part in or witnessed (saw) an historical event are called *primary sources*. Can historians believe everything they read in a primary source? Explain.

Things to Do

1. Be an Arawak in 1492. Working with three other classmates, write a response to Columbus's account on pages 73–74.
2. Working in a group with three other students, and using the documents in this unit as your source, write your own account of the Columbus–Arawak encounter. Then answer these questions:

   a. In what ways is your account limited?
   b. What can you do that would make your account less limited?
   c. Are historical accounts always limited no matter how many documents, artifacts, and resources the historian has? Why or why not?
   d. What conclusions can you make about the writing of historical accounts based on this activity?

3. Carl Becker, the famous historian, said that every person was his or her own historian. What did he mean? To what extent is his statement accurate?

Teaching about Revolutions Using Social Science Inquiry

Social Science Inquiry

In the unit on revolutions described below, Ms. Garcia, a senior high school social studies teacher, uses the inquiry model illustrated in Figure 6.2 (page 71) to teach a powerful concept: *revolution*. She uses three American revolutions as content samples: (1) the Pueblo Revolution in 1680, in which the Pueblo tribes of New Mexico revolted against the Spanish; (2) the revolution in the British Colonies (1776); and (3) the Mexican Revolution of 1810.

Creating Doubt and Concern: Motivating Students

Ms. Garcia starts the unit by having the class play the simulation game, *Starpower* (Shirts, 1969). In this game, after a round of trading chips, the players are divided into three groups according to the number of points they have: the *squares* (with the most points), the *circles* (with the least points), and the *triangles* (those in between). Ms. Garcia then distributes the chips in such a way that, without the players knowing it, will keep the squares ahead of the other two groups.

A highly stratified society is created with little opportunity for mobility. When they are in a clearly dominant position, Ms. Garcia gives the squares the power to make the rules of the game. They make rules that help to keep themselves in power. The circles and the triangles become very angry and frustrated and call the rules dictatorial and fascist. The frustrations become so high that the game ends in a revolt against the rules and the squares.

Formulating Questions and Hypotheses

Ms. Garcia uses the simulation game as a vehicle to start the unit on revolutions and to get the students to formulate questions related to the rise of pre-revolutionary conditions in a society. She asks the students:

1. Why did the circles and the triangles become so angry and frustrated?
2. Have you ever had a real-life experience in which you felt this way? If so, what was it? Why did you feel that way? What did you do about it?
3. How did the simulation game end? Why did it end that way?
4. Can you think of examples of people and groups in history and in modern times who felt the way the triangles and circles felt at the end of the game?

Through questions and cues, Ms. Garcia gets the students to discuss these examples: (1) the Pilgrims in 17th-century England, who were opposed to the Church of England; (2) the American colonists in the late 1700s, who were angry with Britain about taxation without representation; (3) the Cherokee Indians in the Southeast in the 1830s, who were forced to move from their homeland to Oklahoma; (4) the Jews in Germany in the 1930s and 1940s, who experienced discrimination and persecution; and (5) African Americans in the South during the 1950s and 1960s, who experienced discrimination.

Ms. Garcia asks: What kinds of conditions made these groups angry? (Ms. Garcia is trying to get the students to state *hypotheses* about conditions that can lead to anger and rebellion.) The class keeps a list of its statements about the kinds of conditions that made these groups so angry.

Ms. Garcia asks the students to list some things that individuals and groups might be able to do when they feel like the triangles and the circles, as did the Jews in Germany in the 1930s and 1940s, or the American colonists in 1776. The students state that these groups might (1) let the authorities know how unhappy they are, (2) try to change the laws and rules, or (3) migrate to another place or nation.

Ms. Garcia then asks: What if none of these things is possible? What if none of them helps to improve the conditions of those who feel mistreated? Then what might they do? Through continual questioning, cues, and examples, Ms. Garcia helps the students to state that if all efforts fail to improve their conditions, then groups might try to overthrow the government, if certain conditions prevail.

Ms. Garcia tells the class that, depending on many conditions within a society, a group that feels mistreated may do many different things, including start a protest movement, migrate, start riots, and, in particular cases, try to overthrow the government. She points out that in most of the examples the class discussed, the groups did not try to overthrow the government. She asks: What particular conditions do you think must exist before a group that is very angry tries to overthrow the government? (Ms. Garcia is trying to get the students to hypothesize about the causes of revolutions.) The class keeps a list of the hypotheses it states.

Ms. Garcia asks the students to give their ideas about what they think happens when the old government is overthrown and a new government is established. (Ms. Garcia is trying to get the students to state hypotheses about what happens when a revolution occurs and a new government is established.) The class keeps a record of its hypotheses.

Ms. Garcia helps the students to summarize the major questions they have raised and will study during the unit:

1. What kinds of things make groups very angry within a nation or society?
2. What kinds of things do groups do when they are very angry about the way in which the government and officials of a nation are treating them?
3. Under what conditions will groups try to overthrow the government when they feel angry and mistreated?
4. What happens when the government is overthrown?
5. Does the new government remove the conditions that cause the old government to be overthrown?

Defining Concepts

Ms. Garcia tells the class that it has discussed two major ideas that social scientists use specific concepts to describe. The powerlessness and frustration that the triangles and circles felt at the end of the simulation is called *alienation* by sociologists. Alienated individuals and groups feel that they cannot control their destiny or have any significant influence on the important events within their society (Marshall, 1994). She tells the students that when the government of a nation is suddenly overthrown and a new government is established, a revolution has taken place. She gives the students Crane Brinton's (1962) definition of a revolution: "The drastic, sudden substitution of one group in charge of the running of a territorial political entity for another group" (p. 4).

Ms. Garcia tells the class that the word *revolution* is used in many different ways. (Ms. Garcia gives examples of it, meaning a complete change in something.) She says that in this unit it will be used to mean the sudden replacement of one government by another.

Collecting Data

Ms. Garcia decides to use a combination of lectures, class discussions, and small groups to present and gather data. Drawing on materials primarily from the French Revolution of 1789, Ms. Garcia presents several lectures in which she sketches some of the major reasons that revolutions develop, some of their major characteristics, and what often happens in the postrevolutionary period. Each of her lectures is followed by a discussion session in which she asks the students higher-level questions that help them to develop concepts and generalizations about the characteristics of a revolution and the conditions under which they occur.

Ms. Garcia divides the class into three groups to do independent research on three American revolutions: the Pueblo Revolution in 1680; the Revolution in the English Colonies in 1776; and the Mexican Revolution in 1810.

The class develops the data retrieval chart in Table 6.3 to guide the research of each group.

Ms. Garcia also plans some total class data-gathering activities in addition to her lectures. The students read Chapters 1, 2, and 9 in *The Anatomy of Revolution* by Crane Brinton (1962). In this book, Brinton derives generalizations about revolutions by analyzing four: the English (1649), the American (1776), the French (1789), and the Russian (1917). The students also read George Orwell's (1946) *Animal Farm*, a disguised political satire of the Russian revolution.

Evaluating Data and Deriving Generalizations

When the three research groups collect their data, they analyze the results, making sure that they answer all of the questions in Table 6.3. Each of the

TABLE 6.3   Data Retrieval Chart on Revolutions

Questions	Pueblo Revolution 1680	American Revolution 1776	Mexican Revolution 1810
Who were the people or groups in power?			
What people or groups wanted power?			
What were the major causes of the revolution?			
What incident(s) triggered the revolution?			
What was gained or lost and by whom?			
What happened immediately afterward?			
What happened in the long run?			

three groups presents its findings to the class in a different format. The group that studies the Pueblo Revolution presents its findings to the class in the form of a dramatization. A narrator describes the highlights of the revolution as the other students in the group act them out. This group describes how the Pueblo Revolution ultimately failed when the Pueblos were reconquered by the Spanish:

> Pope was dead. The Pueblo tribes had tired of fighting. They were ill and hungry. Vargas brought an army of less than a hundred soldiers to Santa Fe in 1692. Tall, sure of himself and quiet in his manner, he took the town without fighting. Then he went from pueblo to pueblo convincing the Indians once again to accept Spanish rule, never firing a shot. In this way he "conquered" 73 Pueblos for the Spanish.

The English Colonies group prepares a striking mural that depicts the major events in that revolution. The students share this mural when making their class presentation. The Mexican Revolution group presents its findings to the class in a panel discussion.

During and after each group's presentation, using the data retrieval chart in Table 6.3, the class formulates generalizations about the three revolutions. The class discusses ways in which the three revolutions were alike and different. The Pueblo Revolution was the most different from the other two in that it ultimately failed because the Pueblo tribes were eventually reconquered by the Spaniards. The students compare the generalizations they developed with those stated by Brinton in the last chapter of *The Anatomy of Revolution*. They also compare their findings with the view of a revolution presented in Orwell's *Animal Farm* and discuss the extent to which fiction can provide insights into social reality.

When the unit ends, Ms. Garcia not only has succeeded in helping the students to derive concepts and generalizations about revolutions, but she also has helped them gain a keen appreciation for the difficulties historians face in reconstructing historical events, establishing cause and effect, and formulating accurate generalizations.

A Multicultural Math Lesson

I stated in Chapter 3 that math and science teachers should respond to multicultural education mainly by implementing *equity pedagogy* or *culturally responsive* teaching strategies. Equity pedagogy exists when teachers use techniques and teaching methods that facilitate the academic achievement of students from diverse racial, ethnic, and social-class groups.

A number of mathematics educators have developed theoretical and practical work that will help teachers to increase equity in mathematics for all students (Nasir & Cobb, 2007; Secada, Fennema, & Adajian, 1995). Research indicates that culturally responsive teaching strategies can increase student motivation and help students from diverse groups master content in different subjects, including math and science (Au, 2006; González, Moll, & Amanti, 2005; Mahiri, 2004). Treisman (1992) found that the achievement of African Americans in college calculus improved tremendously when he created study groups in which they participated. Groupwork has been found to help students from diverse groups to increase their academic achievement (Cohen, 1994). Although I think that math and science teachers should focus on equity pedagogy and culturally responsive teaching, a part of equity pedagogy and culturally responsive teaching is incorporating multicultural content into instruction in the various subject areas, as the math lesson below illustrates.

Teachers can integrate multicultural content into math by using concepts and examples that have been developed by curriculum developers in ethnomathematics (Addison-Wesley, 1993; Ascher, 1991; Ascher & Ascher, 1981; Powell & Frankenstein, 1997). Ethnomathematics is

> the study of mathematics which takes into consideration the culture in which mathematics arises. Mathematics is often associated with the study of "universals." When we speak of "universals," however, it is important to recognize that often something we think of as universal is merely universal to those who share our cultural and historical perspectives. (*Ethnomathematics*, 2006)

The following sources include multicultural math examples developed by curriculum specialists in ethnomathematics that teachers can incorporate into their math lessons:

> Addison-Wesley (1993). *Multiculturalism in Mathematics, Science, and Technology: Readings and Activities.* Menlo Park, CA: Addison-Wesley.
>
> Ascher, M. (1991). *Ethnomathematics: A Multicultural View of Mathematical Ideas.* Pacific Grove, CA: Brooks/Cole.
>
> Ascher, M., & Ascher, R. (1981). *The Code of the Quipu: A Study in Media, Mathematics and Culture.* Ann Arbor, MI: University of Michigan Press.

The lesson below combines groupwork—a strategy that has been used effectively in culturally responsive teaching (Cohen, 1994; Treisman, 1992)—with content related to ethnic groups in order to give students an opportunity to practice math skills and use mathematical knowledge.

Using Immigration Data to Practice Math Knowledge and Skills

Big Idea in Lesson
Math skills can be used to help us to better understand immigration trends to the United States. Social science can help us to interpret those trends.

Lesson Objective
In this lesson, students will use their knowledge and basic skills in math to better understand immigration trends and patterns in the United States.

1. Give the students a copy of Table 6.4, which shows immigration by country to the United States from 1981 to 1998. You may want to simplify this table, depending on the grade level of your students and their prior experiences with reading and interpreting charts and tables. Ask the students to work in groups and construct a chart that shows total immigration figures for immigrants from Asian nations from 1981 to 1998. Also ask them to arrange the chart so that it shows—in descending order—the largest to the smallest group.

TABLE 6.4   Immigrants by Country of Birth: 1981 to 1998 (in thousands; 7,338.1 represents 7,338,100)

Country of birth	1981–1990, total	1991–1996, total	1997	1998
All countries	**7,338.1**	**6,146.2**	**798.4**	**660.5**
Europe [1]	705.6	875.6	119.9	90.8
France	23.1	16.9	2.6	2.4
Germany	70.1	43.7	5.7	5.5
Greece	29.1	1 0.0	1.0	0.9
Ireland	32.8	54.9	1.0	0.9
Italy	32.9	14.7	2.0	1.8
Poland	97.4	130.2	12.0	8.5
Portugal	40.0	17.1	1.7	1.5
Romania	38.9	34.3	5.5	5.1
Soviet Union, former [2]	84.0	339.9	49.1	30.2
Armenia	(NA)	[3]20.8	2.1	1.1
Azerbaijan	(NA)	[3]12.3	1.5	0.5
Belarus	(NA)	[3]21.4	3.1	1.0
Russia	(NA)	[3]70.4	16.6	11.5
Ukraine	(NA)	[3]92.2	15.7	7.4
Uzbekistan	(NA)	[3]16.1	3.3	0.6
United Kingdom	142.1	95.0	10.7	9.0
Yugoslavia	19.2	31.7	10.8	8.0

Country of birth	1981–1990, total	1991–1996, total	1997	1998
Asia [1]	**2,817.4**	**1,941.9**	**265.8**	219.7
Afghanistan	26.6	13.6	1.1	0.8
Bangladesh	15.2	35.4	8.7	8.6
Cambodia	116.6	11.9	1.6	1.4
China	[4]388.8	268.7	41.1	36.9
Hong Kong	63.0	52.9	5.6	5.3
India	261.9	236.5	38.1	36.5
Iran	154.8	79.4	9.6	7.9
Iraq	19.6	26.8	3.2	2.2
Israel	36.3	22.9	2.4	2.0
Japan	43.2	39.9	5.1	5.1
Jordan	32.6	25.1	4.2	3.3
Korea	338.8	114.1	14.2	14.3
Laos	145.6	37.8	1.9	1.6
Lebanon	41.6	29.9	3.6	3.3
Pakistan	61.3	70.5	13.0	13.1
Philippines	495.3	348.5	49.1	34.5
Syria	20.6	16.6	2.3	2.8
Taiwan	([4])	76.8	6.7	7.1
Thailand	64.4	36.1	3.1	3.1
Turkey	20.9	15.7	3.1	2.7
Vietnam	401.4	317.8	38.5	17.6
North America [1]	**3,125.0**	**2,740.7**	**307.5**	**253.0**
Canada	119.2	90.7	11.6	10.2
Mexico	1,653.3	1,651.4	146.9	131.6
Caribbean [1]	892.7	655.4	105.3	75.5
Cuba	159.2	94.9	33.6	17.4
Dominican Republic	251.8	258.1	27.1	20.4
Haiti	140.2	114.4	15.1	13.4
Jamaica	213.8	109.8	17.8	15.1
Trinidad and Tobago	39.5	41.1	6.4	4.9
Central America [1]	458.7	342.8	43.7	35.7
El Salvador	214.6	147.7	18.0	14.6
Guatemala	87.9	70.3	7.8	7.8
Honduras	49.5	41.9	7.6	6.5
Nicaragua	44.1	50.4	6.3	3.5
Panama	29.0	16.9	2.0	1.6
South America [1]	**455.9**	**344.0**	**52.9**	**45.4**
Argentina	25.7	17.1	2.0	1.5

(continued)

TABLE 6.4   Continued

Country of birth	1981–1990, total	1991–1996, total	1997	1998
Brazil	23.7	32.4	4.6	4.4
Chile	23.4	11.4	1.4	1.2
Colombia	124.4	81.7	13.0	11.8
Ecuador	56.0	45.2	7.8	6.9
Guyana	95.4	53.6	7.3	4.0
Peru	64.4	66.7	10.9	10.2
Venezuela	17.9	16.2	3.3	3.1
Africa [1]	**192.3**	**213.1**	**47.8**	**40.7**
Egypt	31.4	28.0	5.0	4.8
Ethiopia	27.2	30.9	5.9	4.2
Ghana	14.9	18.0	5.1	4.5
Nigeria	35.3	37.9	7.0	7.7
South Africa	15.7	14.2	2.1	1.9
Other countries [5]	41.9	31.0	4.5	10.9

NA Not available.

[1] Includes countries not shown separately.

[2] Includes other republics and unknown republics, not shown separately.

[3] Covers years 1992–1996.

[4] Data for Taiwan included with China.

[5] Includes unknown countries.

Source: U.S. Census Bureau (2000), p. 10.

2. Ask the students to list, in a third column in the chart, the percentage of Asian immigrants in each group. Then ask the students to make hypotheses to explain the immigration trends they notice in their chart.

3. Ask the students to work in groups and make a second chart that shows the total number of immigrants from the following continents: Europe, Asia, North America, and Africa. Then ask them to add a column in the chart that shows the percentage of total immigrants to the United States from each continent. Ask them to identify any trends they notice in their chart and to formulate hypotheses to explain these trends.

Skills Practiced in Chart

In making the two charts described above, the students will be practicing a number of math skills, including how to read and interpret charts with statistical data, addition, and the computation of percent, which involves division.

References for This Lesson

Suárez-Orozco, C., & Suárez-Orozco, M. M. (2001). *Children of Immigration*. Cambridge, MA: Harvard University Press.

Suárez-Orozco, M. M., & Páez, M. M. (Eds.). (2002). *Latinos: Remaking America*. Berkeley: University of California Press.

A Multicultural Science Lesson

Concepts in science can be incorporated into the multicultural curriculum and used to help students develop deeper understandings of scientific concepts. Concepts related to the biological basis of skin color and diseases that are more frequent among some population groups than others—such as sickle cell anemia, hypertension, and melanoma—are among the science and health related topics that can be incorporated into the multicultural curriculum. The ways in which science has been used to both support and challenge race and racism are important scientific ideas that can be taught in a multicultural curriculum. This lesson focuses on the ways in which science is embedded within and mirrors its social and political context.

Racial Categories and Scientific Racism

Big Idea in Lesson
Race is an attempt by scientists to structure human groups on the basis of inherited physical characteristics. However, these attempts have been largely unsuccessful. As the term is used today, notions of race are primarily social constructions whose categories change over time and reflect the times and society in which they are created. Some scientists have constructed concepts of race that have helped to justify discrimination against groups with certain biological characteristics.

Lesson Objective
Students will learn that the construction of race reflects the social and historical context, that ideas of race change over time, that the notions of race that scientists construct reflect the times in which they live, and that some conceptions of race that scientists have constructed have helped to justify the discrimination and inequality experienced by some racial and ethnic groups.

1. Ask the students to give their ideas of what racial groups or categories exist. Write their ideas on the board. Then have them compare their ideas of what racial groups exist with definitions and categories of race they can find in a dictionary, an encyclopedia, and on the Internet. The students will discover that the construction of race is an attempt by scientists to categorize human population groups on the basis of their genetically transmitted physical characteristics. However, they will discover by examining the many different categories of racial groups that this is a very difficult task, that there are many different definitions and categories of race and that the definitions and categories change over time.

2. Give the students this definition of race from *The American Heritage College Dictionary* (2002, p. 1147): "A local or global human population distinguished as a more or less distinct group by genetically transmitted physical characteristics."

3. Using information in Gould's (1996) book, *The Mismeasure of Man,* tell the students about scientists in the 1800s who believed that human racial groups had separate origins and that Caucasians were superior to other races (Nott & Gliddon, 1854). These scientists used *craniometry*—the comparative measurement of skulls—to make claims about racial group differences (Gould, 1996). Have students investigate the research and work of Sir Francis Galton (1822 to 1911), the English scientist who was a founder of eugenics and a cousin of Charles Darwin.

4. Share with the students information from Gould (1996) about how intelligence testing—which was developed by researchers such as Lewis M. Terman at Stanford—exemplified many of the ideas about racial differences that had been expressed by the advocates of craniometry after craniometry had been discredited.

5. Ask the students to identify on the Internet and other sources the racial categories used by scientists today compared to those used by the U.S. Census Bureau in 1840, 1850, and 1860. In each of these censuses, a "mulatto" category was included for Blacks who were partly White, although the category was not defined. "Mulattoes" were officially defined in the 1870 and 1880 censuses to include "quadroons, octoroons, and all persons having any perceptible trace of African blood" (Davis, 1991). The mulatto category was dropped in the 1920 census and "black was defined to mean any person with any black ancestry" (Davis, 1991).

6. Have the students investigate the various racial categories that were used to classify White ethnic groups in the early 1900s. Various groups of Whites became distinct races that were ranked, such as the Celtic, Slav, Hebrew, Iberic, Mediterranean, and Anglo-Saxon (Jacobson, 1998). Anglo-Saxon was classified as the superior race. The Dillingham Commission formed to investigate immigration in 1907 concluded that there was a fundamental difference in the character and the causes of the new immigrants from Central, Southern, and Eastern Europe and the old immigrants from Northern and Western Europe. This kind of thinking culminated in the Immigration Act of 1924, which placed extreme quotas on immigrants from Central, Southern, and Eastern Europe and blatantly discriminated against them.

7. Have students investigate the case of Leo Frank. Leo Frank, a Jewish northerner, became a victim of anti-Semitism and racial hostility when he was accused of murdering a White girl who worked in a pencil factory he co-owned in Atlanta, Georgia. In 1915, he was found guilty in an unfair trial. When the governor of Georgia commuted his sentence, a White mob forcibly removed him from jail and lynched him. Point out to the students that Frank was considered Jewish and not White. Show the students the section of the video-tape, *The Long Shadow of Hate*, produced by Teaching Tolerance (a division of the Southern Poverty Law Center), which describes the trial and sentence of Frank.

8. Have the students conclude by stating what generalizations they can make about how racial categories change, the role that scientists play and have played in these changes, and how science reflects the social context in which it takes place.

References for This Lesson

Davis, F. J. (1991). *Who Is Black: One Nation's Definition*. University Park: Pennsylvania State University Press.

Gould, S. J. (1996). *The Mismeasure of Man*. (rev. ed.). New York: Norton.

López, I. F. (1966). *White by Law: The Legal Construction of Race*. New York: New York University Press.

Value Inquiry in the Multicultural Curriculum

The multicultural curriculum should help students to identify, examine, and clarify their values; consider value alternatives; and make reflective value choices they can defend within a society in which human dignity is a shared value. You can use the value inquiry model I developed to help your students to identify and clarify their values and to make reflective moral choices (Banks & Banks, 1999). The Banks value inquiry model consists of the following nine steps:

1. Defining and recognizing value problems
2. Describing value-relevant behavior
3. Naming values exemplified by the behavior
4. Determining conflicting values in behavior described
5. Hypothesizing about the possible consequences of the values analyzed

6. Naming alternative values to those exemplified by behavior observed
7. Hypothesizing about the possible consequences of values analyzed
8. Declaring value preferences: choosing
9. Stating reasons, sources, and possible consequences of value choice: justifying, hypothesizing, predicting

You can use a variety of materials and resources to stimulate value inquiry and discussion of multicultural issues and topics, such as documents similar to the ones used in the historical inquiry lesson described in this chapter, newspaper feature stories, textbook descriptions of issues and events, and open-ended stories such as the one below. When using the open-ended story below, "Trying to Buy a Home in Lakewood Island" (Banks, 2003), you can use the value inquiry model to develop questions like the ones that follow the story to stimulate value discussion and decision making.

Trying to Buy a Home in Lakewood Island

About a year ago, Joan and Henry Green, a young African American couple, moved from the West Coast to a large city in the Midwest. They moved because Henry finished his Ph.D. in chemistry and took a job at a big university in Midwestern City. Since they have been in Midwestern City, the Greens have rented an apartment in the central area of the city. However, they have decided that they want to buy a house. Their apartment has become too small for the many books and other things they have accumulated during the year. In addition to wanting more space, they also want a house so that they can receive breaks on their income tax, which they do not receive living in an apartment. The Greens also think that a house will be a good financial investment.

The Greens have decided to move into a suburban community. They want a new house and most of the houses within the city limits are rather old. They also feel that they can obtain a larger house for their money in the suburbs than in the city. They have looked at several suburban communities and have decided that they like Lakewood Island better than any of the others. Lakewood Island is a predominantly White community, which is composed primarily of lower-middle-class and middle-class residents. There are a few wealthy families in Lakewood Island. But they are the exceptions rather than the rule.

Joan and Henry Green have become frustrated because of the problems they have experienced trying to buy a home in Lakewood Island. Before they go out to look at a house, they carefully study the newspaper ads. When they arrived at the first house in which they were interested, the owner told them that his house had just been sold. A week later they decided to work with a realtor. When they tried to close the deal on the next house they wanted, the realtor told them that the owner had raised the price $40,000 because he had the house appraised since he had put it on the market and had discovered that his selling price was much too low. When the Greens tried to buy a third house in Lakewood Island, the owner told them that he had decided not to sell because he had not received the job in another city that he was almost sure that he would receive when he had put his house up for sale. He explained that the realtor had not removed the ad about his house from the newspaper even though he had told him that he had decided not to sell a week earlier. The realtor the owner had been working with had left the real estate company a few days ago. Henry is bitter and feels that he and his wife are victims of racial discrimination. Joan believes that Henry is paranoid and that they have been the victims of a series of events that could have happened to anyone, regardless of their race. (pp. 217, 219)

1. What is the main problem in the case?
2. What are the values of Joan Green? Henry Green? The realtor? The owners? What behaviors show the values you have listed?
3. How are the values of these individuals alike and different? Why? Joan Green, Henry Green, the realtor, the owners.
4. Why are the values of these individuals alike and different? Joan Green, Henry Green, the realtor, the owners.
5. What are other values that these individuals could embrace? Joan Green, Henry Green, the realtor, the owners.
6. What are the possible consequences of the values and actions of each of these individuals? Joan Green, Henry Green, the realtor, the owners.
7. What should the Greens do?
8. Why should the Greens take this action? What are the possible consequences of the actions you stated above?
9. What would you do if you were the Greens? Why?

Conceptual Teaching and Curriculum Transformation

An important goal of multicultural education is to transform the curriculum so that students develop an understanding of how knowledge is constructed and the extent to which it is influenced by the personal, social, cultural, and gender experiences of knowledge producers (Code, 1991; Collins, 2000; Harding, 1991). Organizing the curriculum around powerful ideas and concepts facilitates the development of teaching strategies and learning experiences that focus on knowledge construction and the development of thinking skills. This chapter has described ways in which a conceptual and transformative multicultural curriculum can be designed and implemented.

School Reform and Intergroup Education

Teachers and administrators for schools of today and tomorrow should acquire the knowledge, attitudes, and skills needed to work with students from diverse cultural groups and to help all students develop positive racial attitudes. Teachers and administrators also need to restructure schools so that they will be able to deal effectively with the growing diversity in the United States and the world and to prepare future citizens who will be able to compete in a global world economy that will be knowledge and service oriented.

The first part of this chapter describes the demographic trends and developments related to the U.S. changing ethnic texture and future workforce, states why school restructuring is essential in order to prepare the workforce needed for the 21st century, and describes the major variables of multicultural school reform.

The second part describes the characteristics of children's racial attitudes and guidelines for helping students to acquire positive racial attitudes, values, beliefs, and actions. This knowledge is essential for the preparation of teachers and administrators who will work in today's culturally, racially, and linguistically diverse schools.

Demographic Trends and the Changing Workforce

The U.S. workforce faces several major problems that have important implications for the professional work of teachers and administrators.

Teachers and administrators need to be aware of these trends and to take part in school reform efforts designed to restructure U.S. schools and institutions of higher education so that they will be able to respond to these demographic trends sensitively and reflectively. I call these trends the *demographic imperative.*

The United States will have a large number of people retiring and too few new workers entering the workforce during the next few decades. The U.S. population is also becoming increasingly older. In 1980, about 12.5 percent of the nation's population consisted of people over age 65. By 2030, 22 percent of the nation's population will be in that age group (Richman, 1990). The cost of supporting older workers will continue to mount in the coming decades. We will be dependent on fewer workers to provide social security funds for retirees. In the boom years of the 1950s, 17 workers supported every retiree. The ratio now is about 2.7 workers to one retiree (Toossi, 2002). Persons of color will account for nearly 47 percent of the labor force by 2050 (Toossi, 2002). If the education of students of color does not improve significantly and quickly, a large number of the workers depended on to contribute to the incomes of retired workers will not have the skills and knowledge to participate effectively in a workforce that will be knowledge and service oriented.

The U.S. economy is becoming increasingly global. Foreign investment in the United States grew from $90 billion in 1980 to $811,756 billion in 1998 (U.S. Census Bureau, 2000). According to the Bureau of Economic Analysis (2006), "In 2004, total accumulated foreign direct investment (FDI) in the United States was $1.5 trillion on a historical cost basis, or some $2.7 trillion at today's market value. This represents approximately 10% of the total current market value of all publicly traded firms." The United States, as well as the other modernized nations, has moved from agricultural, to industrial, to knowledge/service societies. Friedman (2005) calls the world in which we live a flat world because workers educated in Seattle, London, and Paris must compete with those educated in New Delhi, India, and Karachi, Pakistan. Technology makes it possible for companies to send jobs to developing nations where they can be done much cheaper than in the Western developed nations. Most of the new wealth created today is in service industries (Johnson & Packer, 1987). Moreover, employers in Western nations do not limit their search for skilled knowledge workers within the boundaries of their nations. Workers in Western developed nations have to compete with skilled knowledge workers around the world.

People of color will constitute an increasingly larger percentage of the workforce as we move further into the 21st century. Whites made up 70 percent of the labor force in 2006 (U.S. Department of Labor, 2006). Their share of the labor force will decrease gradually and constitute about 65.6 percent of the labor force by 2014 (U.S. Department of Labor, 2006).

If these labor trends continue, there will be a mismatch between the knowledge and skill demands of the workforce and the knowledge and skills of a large proportion of U.S. workers. In 1998, about 26 percent of the labor force was made up of people of color. Their percentage of the workforce will gradually increase in the coming decades. Asian American and Hispanic workers are projected to increase more rapidly than other groups—40 percent and 37 percent respectively—because of their high immigration rates and average fertility (U.S. Department of Labor, 2006). In 2014, Hispanics are projected to make up about 16 percent of the labor force; Asians, 5 percent; and African Americans, 12 percent (Toossi, 2005).

Knowledge-oriented service jobs—in fields such as education, health, and trade—require high-level reasoning and analytical, quantitative, and communication skills. Most corporations today have a transnational identity and find skilled workers to complete required jobs in any nation or part of the world. In a segment of the PBS series *Learning in America*, it was revealed that a New York insurance company was sending paperwork by plane to Dublin at regular intervals to be done by workers there because the company regarded these workers as more competent than comparable workers in the United States. This U.S. insurance company was sending work to Dublin to be done at the same time that the unemployment rate among African American teenagers was as high as 30 to 40 percent in some inner-city communities.

The sending of work abroad foreshadows a trend that is likely to escalate in the future and pose serious problems for the development of productive citizens among ethnic groups of color in the United States. There is a growing need for highly skilled and technical workers in the United States and throughout the world. Yet, if the current levels of educational attainments among most U.S. youths of color continue, the United States will be hard pressed to meet its labor needs with its own citizens. In 2004, 23.8 percent of Hispanic youths and 11.8 percent of African American youths between the ages of 16 and 24 had dropped out of high school, compared to 6.8 percent of White youths and 10.3 percent of all youths (NCES, 2006b). There will be a mismatch between the skills of a large percentage of the workers in the United States and the needs of the labor force.

Scientific, technical, and service jobs will be ample, but the potential workers—about one-third of whom will be people of color—will not have the knowledge and skills to do the jobs. This will occur because of the increasingly large percentage of the school-age population that will be youths of color by 2020 (about 46 percent) and the low quality of the elementary and secondary education that a large number of youths of color are receiving.

There will be an insufficient number of Whites—and particularly White males—to meet U.S. labor demands in the next few decades. Consequently, to meet workforce demands, women and people of color will have to enter scientific and technical fields in greater numbers. In 2003, foreign-born science and engineering students earned one-third of all Ph.D. degrees awarded in the United States (NFS, 2006). *Time* magazine wrote in its September 11, 1989, issue, "The science deficit threatens America's prosperity and possibly even its national security."

Whites are a diminishing percentage of new entrants to the U.S. labor force and of the nation's population because of the low birthrate among Whites and the small proportion of immigrants to the United States who are coming from Europe. In 2003, 78.3 percent of the documented immigrants to the United States came from Latin America (53.3 percent) and Asia (25 percent) and 13.7 percent came from Europe (U.S. Census Bureau, 2004).

The United States is experiencing its largest wave of immigrants since the period from 1880 to 1924, when many Southern, Eastern, and Central European immigrants came to this land. About one million immigrants entered the United States each year during the peak years of the 1990s. Because of the low birthrate among Whites, the large influx of immigrants from Asia and Latin America, and the high birthrates among these groups, the White percentage of the U.S. population is experiencing very little growth.

Between 2000 and 2010, the non-Hispanic White population is projected to increase by 2.7 percent, compared to 34.5 percent for Hispanics, 35.9 percent for Asians and Pacific Islanders, and 11.9 percent for African Americans (U.S. Census Bureau, 2000). Hispanics are one of the nation's fastest-growing groups. They increased from about 22 million in 1990 to more than 35 million in 2000 (U.S. Census Bureau, 2000). The Hispanic population is projected to grow by 187.9 percent between 2000 and 2050, compared to 48.8 percent for the total U.S. population, 32.4 percent for Whites, 212.9 percent for Asians, and 71.3 percent for African Americans (U.S. Census Bureau, 2006b).

In 2005, people of color made up 30.6 percent of the U.S. population (U.S. Census Bureau, 2006a). The growth in the nation's percentage of people of color is expected to outpace the growth in the percentage of Whites into the foreseeable future. The U.S. Census Bureau (2000) projects that Whites and people of color will each constitute about 50 percent of the U.S. population in 2050.

School Reform

Restructuring Schools

An important implication of the demographic and social trends described above is that a major goal of education must be to help low-income students, linguistic minority students, and students of color to develop the knowledge, attitudes, and skills needed to participate in the mainstream workforce and society in this century. This goal is essential but is not sufficient—nor is it possible to attain, in my view, without restructuring educational institutions and institutionalizing new goals and ideals within them. We must also rethink the goals of U.S. society and nation-state if the Untied States is to become a strong, democratic, and just society.

I do not believe that U.S. schools, as they are currently structured, conceptualized, and organized, will be able to help most students of color and linguistic minority students—especially those who are poor and from cultures that differ from the school culture in significant ways—to acquire the knowledge, attitudes, and skills needed to function effectively in the knowledge society in this century. U.S. schools were designed for a different population, at a time when immigrant and poor youths did not need to be literate or have basic skills to get jobs and to become self-supporting citizens (Graham, 2005). When large numbers of immigrants entered the United States in the early 1900s, jobs in heavy industry were available that required little formal knowledge or skills. Thus, the school was less important as a job preparatory institution.

To help future citizens become effective and productive citizens in this century, U.S. schools must be restructured. By restructuring, I mean a *fundamental examination of the goals, values, and purposes of schools and a reconstruction of them*. When restructuring occurs, the total system is recognized as the problem and is the target of reform (Darling-Hammond, 1997). Incremental and piecemeal changes are viewed as insufficient as a reform strategy.

To restructure schools, we need educational leaders who have a vision and who are transformative in orientation. In his influential book, *Leadership,* Burns (1978) identifies two types of leaders: *transformative* and *transactional*. Transformative leaders have a vision that they use to mobilize people to action. This is in contrast to transactional leadership, which is quid pro quo: "If you scratch my back, I will scratch yours." Transactional leadership, which is pervasive within our educational institutions and the larger society, is not motivating people to act and is not resulting in the kinds of changes that we need to respond to the demographic imperative described above. To respond to the demographic imperative, we need transformative leaders who have a vision of the future and the skills and abilities to communicate that vision to others.

Schools must help youths from diverse cultures and groups to attain the knowledge, attitudes, and skills needed to function effectively in this century. To attain this goal, the school must change many of its basic assumptions and practices. School restructuring is essential because the dominant approaches, techniques, and practices used to educate students do not, and I believe will not, succeed with large numbers of students of color, such as African Americans, Native Americans, and Latinos. Most current school practices are having little success with these students for many complex reasons, including negative perceptions and expectations of them that are held by many teachers and administrators (Green, 2000; Valdés, 2001; Valenzuela, 1999). Many of the adults in the lives of these students have little faith in their ability, and many of the students—who have internalized these negative views—have little faith in themselves.

Many of these students are socialized in families and communities where they have seen a lot of failure, misery, and disillusionment (Anyon, 2005). Many of them have seen or experienced little success, especially success that is related to schooling and education. One high school teacher asked a group of his students to write about their successes and failures. One of his Native American students told him that he could not write about success but that he could write easily and at length about failure because he had experienced so much of it. The student then wrote a poignant and moving essay about the daunting failures that he had experienced in his short life.

Increasing Academic Achievement

To help students of color and low-income students to experience academic success, and thus to become effective citizens, the school must be restructured so that these students will have successful experiences within a nurturing, personalized, and caring environment. Some fundamental reforms will have to occur in schools for this kind of environment to be created. Grouping practices that relegate a disproportionate number of low-income students and students of color to lower-tracked classes in which they receive an inferior education will have to be dismantled (Oakes, 2005). A norm will have to be institutionalized within the school that states that all students can and will learn, regardless of their home situations, race, social class, or ethnic group.

The theories and techniques developed by researchers such as Brookover and his colleagues (Brookover et al., 1979; Brookover & Erickson, 1969), Edmonds (1986), and Comer (2004) can help schools bring about the structural changes needed to implement the idea within a school that all children can and will learn. The significant work done in the effective schools movement during the 1970s and 1980s provides important lessons about the powerful role schools can play in increasing the academic achievement of low-income and minority students (Levine & Lezotte, 2001).

The whole-school reforms projects that have been implemented within the last two decades are also sources of rich ideas about ways to increase the academic and social achievement of students of color

and low-income students. The whole-school reforms include Acceler-
ated Schools; the Algebra Project, directed by Robert P. Moses (Moses &
Cobb, 2001); the Comer School Development Program (Comer, 2004);
and Success for All, developed by Robert E. Slavin and his colleagues at
Johns Hopkins University (Slavin & Madden, 2001). A helpful reference
on these reforms is a special issue of the *Journal of Education for Students
Placed at Risk* (Boykin & Slavin, 2000).

Innovative ways need to be devised that involve joint parent-school
efforts in the education of ethnic and linguistic minority students. Most
parents want their children to experience success in school, even though
they may have neither the knowledge nor the resources to actualize their
aspirations for their children. Successful educational interventions with
low-income students and students of color are more likely to succeed if
they have a parent involvement component, as Comer (2004) has dem-
onstrated with his successful interventions in inner-city, predominantly
Black schools. Because of the tremendous changes that have occurred in
U.S. families within the last two decades, we need to rethink and reconceptualize what parent involvement means and to formulate new ways
to involve parents at a time when large numbers of school-age youths are
from single-parent or dual-income families (C. A. M. Banks, 2005).

Empowering Teachers

To restructure schools in a way that increases their ability to educate low-
income youths and youths of color, classroom teachers must be nurtured,
empowered, and revitalized. Disempowered, alienated, underpaid, and
disaffected teachers cannot help students who are victimized by poverty
and discrimination to master the knowledge and skills they need to participate effectively in mainstream society in the 21st century.

Many of the teachers in U.S. schools—especially those who work
in inner-city schools with large numbers of low-income students, students of color, and linguistic minority students—are victimized by societal forces similar to those that victimize their students. Many of these
teachers are underpaid, held in low esteem by elites in society, treated
with little respect by the bureaucratic and hierarchical school districts
in which they work, are the victims of stereotypes, and are blamed for
many problems that are beyond their control. The standards movement,
with its focus on high-stakes testing and accountability, has increased
the sense of victimization felt by many teachers in the nation's inner-city
and low-income schools (Meier & Wood, 2005; Sleeter, 2005).

It is unreasonable to expect disempowered and victimized teachers
to empower and motivate disaffected youths of color. Consequently, major goals of school restructuring must be to give teachers respect, to provide them the ability and authority to make decisions that matter, and

to hold them accountable as professionals for the decisions they make. School reform will succeed only if we treat teachers in ways that we have long admonished them to treat their students. We must have high expectations for teachers, involve them genuinely in decision making, stop teacher bashing, and treat them in a caring and humane way. Only when teachers feel empowered and honored will they have the will and ability to treat with respect and caring students that society has victimized.

The Need for Societal Reform

Teachers and administrators should have the knowledge and skills needed to help students become change agents within society. Education should not just educate students to fit into the existing workforce and the current societal structure. Citizenship education in a multicultural society should have as an important goal helping all students to develop the knowledge, attitudes, and skills needed not only to participate within our society but also to help reform and reconstruct it (Freire, 2000). Problems such as racism, sexism, poverty, and inequality are widespread and permeate many U.S. institutions, including the workforce, the courts, and the schools. To educate future citizens merely to fit into and not to change society will result in the perpetuation and escalation of these problems, including the widening gap between the rich and the poor, racial conflict and tension, and a growing number of people who are victims of poverty and homelessness.

A society that has sharp divisions between the rich and the poor, and between Whites and people of color, is not a stable one. It contains stresses and tensions that can lead to societal upheavals and racial polarization and conflict. Thus, education for the 21st century must not only help students to become literate and reflective citizens who can participate productively in the workforce, but it must also teach them to care about other people in their communities and to take personal, social, and civic action to create a more humane and just society (Banks, 2006c).

Democratic Racial Attitudes and Behaviors

Diversity: An Opportunity and a Challenge

The previous section of this chapter focuses on the need for school reform to increase the academic achievement of all students, especially the achievement of students of color and low-income youth who experience many academic problems. Another important goal of multicultural education is to reduce prejudice among all students and to help them to develop democratic attitudes, beliefs, and actions. This section describes the nature of children's racial attitudes and offers guidelines for helping students to develop positive racial attitudes, beliefs, and actions.

Diversity presents both opportunities and challenges to democratic societies and to teachers. Diversity enriches nations, communities, schools, and classrooms. Individuals from many different racial, ethnic, and cultural groups have made and continue to make significant contributions to U.S. society. Diversity provides a society with myriad and enriched ways to identify, describe, and solve social, economic, and political problems.

Diversity also poses serious challenges to nations, schools, and teachers. Research indicates that students come to school with many stereotypes, misconceptions, and negative attitudes toward outside racial, ethnic, and social-class groups (Stephan & Vogt, 2004). Without curriculum intervention by teachers, the racial attitudes and behaviors of students become more negative and harder to change as they grow older (Aboud & Doyle, 1996; Van Ausdale & Feagin, 2001). An important aim of schools is to provide students with experiences and materials that will help them become thoughtful and active citizens. In a diverse democratic society, effective citizens have positive attitudes and behaviors toward individuals from different racial, ethnic, social-class, and language groups; engage in deliberation with these individuals; and participate in equal-status contact situations with them (Banks, 1993, 2001).

The Contact Hypothesis

Most of the theory and research in social psychology related to race relations has been guided by the *contact hypothesis* and related research that emerged out of the events surrounding World War II. Nazi anti-Semitism and its devastating consequences motivated social scientists in the postwar years to devote considerable attention to theory and research related to improving intergroup relations. The contact hypothesis that guides most of the research and theory in intergroup relations today emerged from the classic works by Williams (1947) and Allport (1954). Allport (1954) states that contact between groups will improve intergroup relations when the contact is characterized by these four conditions: (1) equal status; (2) common goals; (3) intergroup cooperation; and (4) support of authorities, law, and custom.

Cooperative Learning and Interracial Contact

Since the 1970s, a group of investigators have accumulated an impressive body of research on the effects of cooperative learning groups and activities on students' racial attitudes, friendship choices, and achievement. Much of this research has been conducted as well as reviewed by investigators such as Aronson and his colleagues (Aronson & Bridgeman, 1979; Aronson & Gonzalez, 1988), Cohen and her colleagues (Cohen, 1972, 1984a, b; Cohen & Roper, 1972; Cohen & Lotan, 1995), Johnson and Johnson (1981, 1991), Slavin (1979, 1983, 1985), and Slavin and Madden (1979). Schofield (2001) has written an informative review of this research. Most of it has been conducted using elementary and high school students as subjects (Slavin, 1983, 1985).

The research on cooperative learning and interracial contact that has been conducted since 1970 is grounded on Allport's (1954) contact hypothesis. This research lends considerable support to the postulate that cooperative interracial contact situations in schools, if the conditions stated by Allport are present, have positive effects on both student interracial behavior and student academic achievement (Aronson & Gonzalez, 1988; Slavin, 1979, 1983). In his review of 19 studies of the effects of cooperative learning methods, Slavin (1985) found that 16 had positive effects on interracial friendships. In a 2001 review, Slavin describes the positive effects of cooperative groups on cross-racial friendships, racial attitudes, and behavior.

Most of this research supports these postulates: (1) students of color and White students have a greater tendency to make cross-racial friendship choices after they have participated in interracial learning teams such as the jigsaw (Aronson & Bridgeman, 1979) and the Student Teams-Achievement Divisions (STAD) (Slavin, 1979); and (2) the academic achievement of students of color such as African Americans and Mexican Americans is increased when cooperative learning activities are used, while the academic achievement of White students remains about the same in both cooperative and competitive learning situations (Aronson & Gonzalez, 1988; Slavin, 1985). Investigators have also found that cooperative learning methods have increased student motivation and self-esteem (Slavin, 1985) and helped students to develop empathy (Aronson & Bridgeman, 1979).

An essential characteristic of effective cooperative learning groups and methods is that the students experience *equal status* in the contact situation (Allport, 1954). Cohen (1972) has pointed out that both African American and White students may expect and attribute higher status to Whites in an initial interracial contact situation that may perpetuate White dominance. Cohen and Roper (1972) designed an intervention to change this expectation. They taught African American children to build transistor radios and to teach this skill to White students. The Black children taught the White children to build the radios after the children watched a videotape showing the African American children building radios. When interracial work groups were structured, equal status was achieved only in those groups in which the African American children taught the White students to build radios. The White children dominated in the other groups.

The research by Cohen and Roper (1972) indicates that equal status between groups in interracial situations has to be constructed by teachers rather than assumed. If students from diverse racial, ethnic, and language groups are mixed without structured interventions that create equal status conditions in the contact situation, racial and ethnic conflict and categorization are likely to increase. In a series of perceptive and carefully designed studies that span two decades, Cohen and her colleagues (Cohen, 1984a, b; Cohen & Roper, 1972; Cohen & Lotan, 1995) have consistently found that contact among different groups without deliberate interventions to increase equal status and positive interactions among them will increase rather than reduce intergroup tensions. Cohen (1994) has developed practical guidelines and strategies that can be used by teachers to create equal status within racially, culturally, and linguistically diverse classrooms.

Curriculum Interventions

There is a great deal of discussion but little agreement about what constitutes equal status in intergroup contact situations. Some researchers interpret equal status to mean equal socioeconomic status. For example, in his summary of favorable and unfavorable conditions that influence interracial contact, Amir (quoted in Hewstone & Brown, 1986) describes this situation as an unfavorable condition: "In the case of contact between a majority and a minority group, when the members of the minority group are of lower status or are lower in any relevant characteristics than the members of the majority groups." (p. 7) Yet Cohen and Roper (1972) interpret equal status differently. Although the African Americans and White students in their study were from different social-class groups, they created equal role status in the classroom by modifying the perceptions that students held of each racial group. They accomplished this task by assigning the African American students a task that increased their status in the classroom. Cohen and Roper had a *social psychological*, rather than an *economic*, view of equal status.

The representations of different ethnic, racial, and language groups that are embedded in curriculum materials and textbooks—and within the activities and teaching strategies of instructors—privilege some groups of students (thus increasing their classroom status) and erode the status of other students by reinforcing their marginal status in the larger society. Studies of textbooks indicate that the images of groups in textbooks reflect those that are institutionalized within the larger society (Sleeter & Grant, 1991). If we view status from a social psychological perspective, as Cohen and Roper (1972) do, a multicultural curriculum that presents representations of diverse groups in realistic and complex ways can help to equalize the status of all groups within the classroom or school. Readers can see Stephan (1985) and Banks (1993, 2001) for comprehensive reviews of curriculum intervention studies.

Since the 1940s, a number of curriculum intervention studies have been conducted to determine the effects of teaching units and lessons, multiethnic materials, role-playing, and other kinds of simulated experiences on the racial attitudes and perceptions of students. These studies indicate that under certain conditions curriculum interventions can help students develop more positive racial and ethnic attitudes. They provide guidelines that can help teachers improve intergroup relations in their classrooms and schools.

Trager and Yarrow (1952) examined the effects of a democratic curriculum on the racial attitudes of children in the first and second grades. They found that it had a positive effect on the attitudes of both students and teachers. White second-grade children developed more positive racial attitudes after using multiethnic readers in a study conducted by Litcher and Johnson (1969). In a longitudinal evaluation of the television program *Sesame Street,* Bogatz and Ball (1971) found that children who had watched the program for long periods had more positive racial attitudes toward outgroups than did children who had watched the show for shorter periods.

Weiner and Wright (1973) examined the effects of a simulation on the racial attitudes of third-grade children. They divided a class into orange and green people. The children wore colored armbands that designated their group status. On one day of the intervention the students who wore orange armbands experienced discrimination. On the other day, the children who wore green armbands were the victims. On the third day and again two weeks later, the children expressed less prejudiced beliefs and attitudes.

In an intervention which has now attained the status of a classic, Jane Elliot (cited in Peters, 1987) used simulation to teach her students the pain of discrimination. One day she discriminated against the blue-eyed children in her third-grade class; the next day she discriminated against the brown-eyed children. Elliot's intervention is described in the award-winning documentary *The Eye of the Storm.* Eleven of Elliot's former students returned to Riceville, Iowa, 14 years later and shared their powerful memories of the simulation with their former teacher. This reunion is described in *A Class Divided,* a revealing and important documentary film. Byrnes and Kiger (1990) conducted an experimental study—using university students as subjects—to determine the effects of the kind of simulation for which Elliot had attained fame. Their simulation had positive effects on the attitudes of non-Black students toward Blacks but had no effects on the subjects' "stated level of comfort with Blacks in various social situations, as measured by the Social Distance scale" (p. 351).

In a study of the effects of multiethnic social studies materials on the racial attitudes of Black four-year-old students, Yawkey and Blackwell (1974) found that these materials had positive effects if the materials were discussed or read and discussed along with a related field trip. Research indicates that curriculum interventions such as plays, folk dances, music, role-playing, exclusion from a group, discussion in dyads, and interracial contact can also have positive effects on the racial attitudes of students. A curriculum intervention that consisted of folk dances, music, crafts, and role-playing had a positive effect on the racial attitudes of elementary students in a study conducted by Ijaz and Ijaz (1981) in Canada. Four plays about African Americans, Chinese Americans, Jews, and Puerto Ricans increased racial acceptance and cultural knowledge among fourth-, fifth-, and sixth-grade students in the New York City schools in a study conducted by Gimmestad and DeChiara (1982).

Ciullo and Troiani (1988) found that children who were excluded from a group exercise became more sensitive to the feelings of children from other ethnic groups. McGregor (1993) used meta-analysis to integrate findings and to examine the effects of role-playing and antiracist teaching on reducing prejudice in students. Twenty-six studies were located and examined. McGregor concluded that role-playing and antiracist teaching "significantly reduce racial prejudice, and do not differ from each other in their effectiveness" (p. 215).

Aboud and Doyle (1996) designed a study to determine how children's racial evaluations were affected by talking about racial issues with a friend who had a different level of prejudice than their own. The researchers found that "high-prejudice children became significantly less prejudiced in their evaluations after the discussion. Changes were greater in children whose low-prejudice partner made more statements about cross-racial similarity, along with more positive Black and negative White evaluations" (p. 161). A study by Wood and Sonleitner (1996) indicates that childhood interracial contact has a positive, long-term influence on the racial attitudes and behavior of adults. They found that interracial contact in schools and neighborhoods has a direct and significant positive influence on adult racial attitudes toward African Americans.

Guidelines for Reducing Prejudice in Students

The following guidelines are derived from the research discussed above as well as from three reviews of the research I completed (Banks, 1993, 2001, 2006a):

1. Include positive and realistic images of ethnic and racial groups in teaching materials in a consistent, natural, and integrated fashion.
2. Help children to differentiate the faces of members of outside racial and ethnic groups. The best way to do this is to permeate the curriculum with different faces of members of these groups.
3. Involve children in vicarious experiences with various racial and ethnic groups. For example, use films, videos, DVDs, children's books, recordings, photographs, and other kinds of vicarious experiences to expose children to members of different racial, ethnic, cultural, and language groups. Vicarious experiences are especially important for students in predominantly White, Latino, or African American schools or communities who do not have much direct contact with members of other groups. Research indicates that vicarious experiences can be powerful (Katz & Zalk, 1978; Litcher & Johnson, 1969). However, vicarious experiences with different ethnic and racial groups should acquaint students with many different types of people within these groups.
   4. If you teach in an interracial school, involve children in structured interracial contact situations. However, contact alone does not necessarily help children to develop positive racial attitudes. Effective interracial contact situations must have the characteristics described by Allport (1954) that are listed on page 98.
5. Provide positive verbal and nonverbal reinforcement for the color brown.
6. Involve children from different racial and ethnic groups in cooperative learning activities (Cohen, 1994).

Preparing Students for a Changing, Diverse, and Complex World

The demographic changes that are taking place in the United States and around the world make it essential for teachers and administrators to (1) restructure schools so that students from all ethnic, racial, gender, and social-class groups will have an equal opportunity to learn; and (2) implement prejudice reduction strategies so that all students will develop the knowledge, attitudes, and skills needed to function in an increasingly diverse, tense, and problem-ridden world. Because of the enormous problems within our nation and world, educators cannot be neutral (Edelman, 1992). They can either act to help transform our world or enhance the escalation of our problems by inaction. Each educator must make a choice. What will be yours?

CHAPTER 8

Multicultural Education: For Freedom's Sake

In *The Dialectic of Freedom,* Maxine Greene (1988) asks, "What does it mean to be a citizen of the free world?" It means, she concludes, having the capacity to choose, the power to act to attain one's purposes, and the ability to help transform a world lived in in common with others. An important factor that limits human freedom in a pluralistic society is the cultural encapsulation into which all individuals are socialized. People learn the values, beliefs, and stereotypes of their community cultures (Sen, 2006). Although these community cultures enable individuals to survive, they also restrict their freedom and ability to make critical choices and to take actions to help reform society.

Education within a pluralistic society should affirm and help students understand their home and community cultures (Banks, 2006c). However, it should also help free them from their cultural boundaries (Appiah, 2006; Sen, 2006). To create and maintain a civic community that works for the common good, education in a democratic society should help students acquire the knowledge, attitudes, and skills needed to participate in civic action to make society more equitable and just. Multicultural education is an education for freedom (Parekh, 1986) that is essential in today's ethnically and religiously polarized and troubled world (King, 2006). It has evoked a divisive national debate in part because of the divergent views that citizens hold about what constitutes an American identity and about the roots and nature of American civilization. The debate, in turn, has sparked a power struggle over who should participate in formulating the canon used to shape the curriculum in the nation's schools, colleges, and universities (Graff, 1992; Nussbaum, 2002).

The Debate over the Canon

During the 1990s a chorus of strident voices launched an orchestrated and widely publicized attack on the movement to infuse content about ethnic groups and women into the school, college, and university curriculum. Much of the debate about multicultural education took place in mass media publications such as *Time* (Gray, 1991), *The Wall Street Journal* (Sirkin, 1990), and *The New Republic* (Howe, 1991), rather than in scholarly journals and forums. The Western traditionalists (writers who defend the canon now within the schools and universities) and the multiculturalists rarely engage in reflective dialogue. Rather, scholars on each side of the debate marshal data to support their briefs and ignore facts, interpretations, and perspectives that are inconsistent with their positions and visions of the present and future.

In his book *Illiberal Education,* D'Souza (1991) defends the Western-centric curriculum and structures in higher education while presenting an alarming picture of where multiculturalism is taking the nation. When multiculturalists respond to such criticism, they often fail to describe the important ways in which the multicultural vision is consistent with the democratic ideals of the West and with the heritage of Western civilization. The multicultural literature pays too little attention to the fact that the multicultural education movement emerged out of Western democratic ideals. One of its major aims is to close the gap between the Western democratic ideals of equality and justice and societal practices that contradict those ideals, such as discrimination based on race, gender, and social class (Feagin & Sikes, 1994; Rothenberg, 2004).

Because so much of the debate over the canon has taken place in the popular media, which encourages simplistic, sound-bite explanations, the issues related to the curriculum canon have been overdrawn and oversimplified by advocates on both sides. The result is that the debate often generates more heat than light. Various interest groups have been polarized rather than encouraged to exchange ideas that might help us find creative solutions to the problems related to race, ethnicity, gender, and schooling. Despite the significant inroads that multicultural education attained in becoming respected and institutionalized during the 1990s, a few strident attacks on it continued into the late 1990s (Stotsky, 1999).

As the ethnic texture of the United States and the world deepens, problems related to diversity will intensify rather than diminish. Consequently, we need leaders and educators of goodwill—from all political and ideological persuasions—to participate in genuine discussions, dialogue, and debates that will help us formulate visionary and workable solutions and enable us to deal creatively with the challenges posed by the increasing diversity in the United States and the world. We must learn how to transform the problems related to racial, ethnic, cultural, language, and religious diversity into opportunities and strengths.

Sharing Power

Western traditionalists and multiculturalists must realize that they are entering into debate from different power positions. Western traditionalists hold the balance of power, financial resources, and the top positions in the mass media; in schools, colleges, and universities; in the government; and in the publishing industry. Genuine discussion between the traditionalists and the multiculturalists can take place only when power is placed on the table, negotiated, and shared.

Despite all of the rhetoric about the extent to which Chaucer, Shakespeare, Milton, and other Western writers are threatened by the onslaught of women and writers of color into the curriculum, the reality is that the curriculum in U.S. schools, colleges, and universities is largely Western in its concepts, paradigms, and content (Bloom, 1994). Concepts such as the Middle Ages and the Renaissance are still used to organize most units in history, literature, and the arts. When content about African and Asian cultures is incorporated into the curriculum, it is usually viewed within the context of European concepts and paradigms. For example, Asian, African, and American histories are often studied under the topic "The Age of Discovery," which means the time when Europeans first arrived in these continents.

Facing Realities

If they are to achieve a productive dialogue rather than a polarizing debate, both Western traditionalists and the multiculturalists must face some facts. The growing number of people of color in U.S. society and schools constitutes a *demographic imperative* educators must hear and respond to. The U.S. Census indicates that in 2000 28 percent of Americans were people of color and projects that they will make up about half of the U.S. population by 2050. Students of color made up about 43 percent of the U.S. public school population in fall 2004 (NCES, 2006a); they are predicted to make up about half of the nation's students by 2020 (Pallas et al., 1989). Although the school and university curricula remain Western oriented, the growing number of people of color will increasingly demand to share power in curriculum decision making and in shaping a curriculum canon that reflects their experiences, histories, struggles, and victories.

People of color, women, and other marginalized groups are demanding that their voices, visions, and perspectives be included in the curriculum. They ask that the debt Western civilization owes to Africa, Asia, and indigenous America be acknowledged (Bernal, 1987, 1991; Lefkowitz & Rogers, 1996; Weatherford, 1991). The advocates of the Afrocentric curriculum—in sometimes passionate language that reflects a dream long deferred—are asking that the cultures of Africa and African American people be legitimized in the curriculum and that the African contributions to European civilization be acknowledged (Asante, 1998; Asante & Mazama, 2005). People of color and women are also demanding that the facts about their victimization be told, not only for truth's sake but also because they need to better understand their conditions so that they and others can work to reform society.

However, these groups must acknowledge that they do not want to eliminate Aristotle and Shakespeare or Western civilization from the school curriculum. To reject the West would be to reject important aspects of their own cultural heritages, experiences, and identities. The most important scholarly and literary works written by African Americans—such as works by W. E. B. DuBois, Carter G. Woodson, and Zora Neale Hurston—are expressions of Western cultural experiences. African American culture resulted from a blending of African cultural characteristics with those of African peoples in the United States (Appiah & Gates, 2005).

Reinterpreting Western Civilization

Rather than excluding Western civilization from the curriculum, multiculturalists want a more truthful, complex, and diverse version of the West taught in the schools. They want the curriculum to describe the ways in which African, Asian, and indigenous American cultures have influenced and interacted with Western civilization. They also want schools to discuss not only the diversity and democratic ideals of Western civilization but also its failures, tensions, and dilemmas, and the struggles by various groups in Western societies to realize their dreams against great odds (Banks, 2003; Takaki, 1993).

We need to deconstruct the myth that the West is homogeneous, that it owes few debts to other world civilizations, and that only privileged and upper-status Europeans and European American males have been its key actors. Weatherford (1988, 1991) describes the debt the West owes to the first Americans. Bernal (1987, 1991), Drake (1987), Sertima (1984), and Clarke (1990) marshal considerable amounts of historical and cultural data that describe the ways in which African and Afroasiatic cultures influenced the development of Western civilization. Bernal, for example, presents linguistic and archaeological evidence to substantiate his claim that important parts of Greek civilization (technologies, language, deities, and architecture) originated in ancient Africa.

We should teach students that knowledge is a *social construction*—that it reflects the perspectives, experiences, and the values of the people and cultures that construct it and is dynamic, changing, and debated among knowledge creators and users (Banks, 1996b, 2006c). Rather than keep such knowledge debates as the extent to which African civilizations contributed to Western civilization out of the classroom, teachers should make them an integral part of teaching (Graff, 1992). The classroom should become a forum in which multicultural debates concerning the construction of knowledge take place. The voices of the Western traditionalists, the multiculturalists, textbook authors, and radical writers should be heard and legitimized in the classroom.

Toward the Democratic Ideal

The fact that multiculturalists want to reformulate and transform the Western canon, not purge the curriculum of the West, is absent from most of the writings of the Western traditionalists. It doesn't support their argument that Shakespeare, Milton, and Aristotle are endangered. By the same token, the multiculturalists have written little about the intersections of multicultural content and a Western-centric canon, perhaps because they have focused on ways in which the established Western canon should be reconstructed and transformed.

Multicultural education itself is a product of the West. It grew out of a struggle guided by Western ideals for human dignity, equality, and freedom (Parker, 2003). Multicultural education is a child of the Civil Rights movement, led by African Americans, which was designed to eliminate discrimination in housing, public accommodation, and other areas. The leaders of the Civil Rights movement—such as Fannie Lou Hamer, Rosa Parks, and Daisy Bates—internalized the American democratic ideal stated in such important U.S. documents as the Declaration of Independence, the Constitution, and the Bill of Rights. The civil rights leaders of the 1960s and 1970s used the Western ideals of freedom and democracy to justify and legitimize their push for structural inclusion and the end of institutionalized discrimination and racism (Branch, 2006).

The Civil Rights movement of the 1960s, led by African Americans, echoed throughout the United States and the world. Other groups—such as Native Americans and Hispanics, women, people with disabilities, and gay rights advocates—initiated their own freedom movements. These cultural revitalization movements made demands on a number of institutions. U.S. schools, colleges, and universities became primary targets for reform, in part because they were important symbols of the structural exclusion that victimized groups experienced and in part because they were easily accessible.

It would be a serious mistake to interpret these cultural revitalization movements and the educational reforms they gave birth to as a repudiation of the West and Western civilization. The major goals of these movements are full inclusion of victimized groups into Western institutions and a reform of these institutions so that their practices are more consistent with their democratic ideals. Multicultural education not only arose out of Western traditions and ideals, but its major goal is to create a nation-state that actualizes the democratic ideals for all that the Founding Fathers intended for an elite few (Franklin, 1976). Rather than being divisive as some critics contend, multicultural education is designed to reduce race, class, and gender divisions in the United States and the world.

Given the tremendous social class and racial cleavages in United States society, it is inaccurate to claim that the study of racial, ethnic, and cultural diversity will threaten national cohesion. The real threats to national unity—which in an economic, sociological, and psychological sense we have not fully attained but are working toward—are the deepening racial and social-class schisms within American society. As Wilson (1999) points out in *The Bridge Over the Racial Divide,* the gap between the rich and the poor has grown tremendously within the last two decades. The social-class schism has occurred not only across racial and ethnic groups but also within these groups. Hence, the rush to the suburbs has not been just a White flight but has been a flight by the middle class of many hues. As a consequence, low-income African Americans and Hispanics have been left in inner-city communities without the middle-class members of their groups to provide needed leadership and role models. They are more excluded than ever from mainstream U.S. society.

Educating for Freedom

Each of us becomes culturally encapsulated during our socialization in childhood. We accept the assumptions of our own community culture, internalize its values, views of the universe, misconceptions, and stereotypes. Although this is as true for the child socialized within a mainstream culture as it is for the minority child, minority children are usually forced to examine, confront, and question their cultural assumptions when they enter school. Students who are born and socialized within the mainstream culture of a society rarely have an opportunity to identify, question, and challenge their cultural assumptions, beliefs, values, and perspectives, because the school culture usually reinforces those that they learn at home and in their communities. Consequently, mainstream Americans have few opportunities to become free of cultural assumptions and perspectives that are monocultural, that devalue African, Asian, and other cultures, and that stereotype people of color and people who are poor or who are victimized in other ways. These mainstream Americans often have an inability to function effectively within other American cultures and lack the ability and motivation to experience and benefit from cross-cultural participation and relationships.

To fully participate in a democratic society, all students need the skills a multicultural education can give them to understand others and to thrive in a rapidly changing, diverse world. Thus, the debate between the Western traditionalists and the multiculturalists fits well within the tradition of a pluralistic democratic society. Its final result will most likely be not exactly what either side wants but a synthesized and compromised perspective that will provide a new vision for survival in the 21st century.

Multicultural Benchmarks

In this chapter, I summarize and highlight the major components of multicultural education. I also describe benchmarks you can use to determine the extent to which your school is multicultural, steps that need to be taken to make it more reflective of cultural diversity, and ways to enhance your school's multicultural climate on a continuing basis. Figure 9.1 summarizes the multicultural benchmarks discussed in this chapter.

A Policy Statement

Your school district needs a policy statement on multicultural education that clearly communicates the board of education's commitment to creating and maintaining schools in which students from both gender groups and from diverse racial, ethnic, social-class, cultural, and language groups will have an equal opportunity to learn.

A cogent board of education policy statement will serve several important purposes. It will give legitimacy to multicultural education in the district and thus facilitate the establishment of programs and practices that foster cultural diversity and equal educational opportunities for all students. A board policy statement will also communicate to parents and the public-at-large that multicultural education is a priority in the district.

The board policy statement should include a rationale or justification for multicultural education and guidelines that can be used by the professional and supportive staffs in the district to develop and implement a comprehensive multicultural education plan. In 1980, the

111

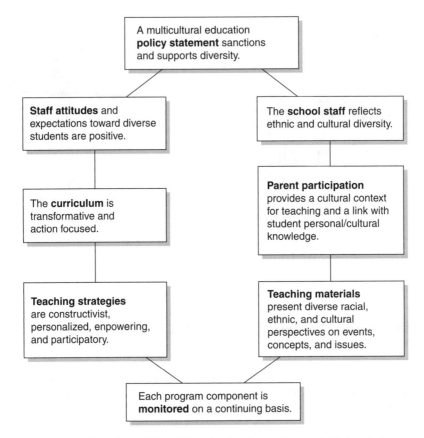

FIGURE 9.1 **Multicultural Benchmarks for Assessing and Maintaining an Effective Multicultural School**

Michigan Department of Education adopted one of the first multicultural education position statements in the United States. It read, in part:

> It is the policy of the State Board of Education that all efforts be made to ac-
> knowledge and recognize that we live in a diverse and multicultural society,
> consisting of racial, ethnic, and religious groups whose cultures, values, be-
> liefs, and lifestyles are valid and viable elements of our democratic society.
> In this context, the State Board of Education fully recognizes the rights of
> persons in the Michigan educational community to learn within the frame-
> work of cultural experiences which maximize the individual development
> of human potential. (p. 4)

In the policy statement adopted by the New York (City) Board of Education (1989), the rationale includes these statements:

Whereas, people from all parts of the world live and work in New York City, necessitating a multicultural education which fosters intergroup knowledge and understanding and equips students to function effectively in a global society; and Whereas, multicultural education values cultural pluralism and rejects the view that schools should seek to melt away cultural differences or merely tolerate cultural diversity; rather, multicultural education accepts cultural diversity as a valuable resource that should be preserved and extended.

In 1996, the Indianapolis Public Schools adopted a multicultural education policy similar to those issued by the Michigan Department of Education and the New York Board of Education. The Indianapolis policy includes rationale statements as well as three major objectives for multicultural education in the district:

1. To promote and foster intergroup understanding, awareness and appreciation by students and staff of the diverse ethnic, racial, cultural, and linguistic groups represented in the Indianapolis Public Schools, the United States, and the world.
2. To help students develop more positive attitudes toward cultural diversity, especially in early grades by dispelling misconceptions, stereotypes, and negative beliefs about themselves and others.
3. To identify the impact of racism and other barriers to acceptance of differences.

In 1992 the Nebraska legislature enacted a multicultural education bill that required the state's public schools to implement multicultural education in all core curriculum areas, kindergarten through 12th grade. The act required the existing curriculum to incorporate content about the histories and cultures of African Americans, Hispanic Americans, Native Americans, and Asian Americans. The bill required that "each school district, in consultation with the State Department of Education, shall develop for incorporation into all phases of the curriculum of grades kindergarten through twelve a multicultural education program." It provided that the state department of education "shall create and distribute recommended multicultural education curriculum guidelines to all school districts. Each district shall create its own multicultural program based on such recommended guidelines."

Your school district can model its multicultural policy statement on those developed by the Michigan Department of Education, the New York Board of Education, the Indianapolis Public Schools, and the Nebraska legislature. Other helpful resources for multicultural education rationales are the position statements developed by national professional organizations such as the *Curriculum Guidelines for Multicultural Education,* a policy statement adopted by the National Council for the Social Studies (NCSS) (Banks, Cortes, Gay, Garcia, & Ochoa, 1992). The rationale for the NCSS guidelines includes these principles:

1. Ethnic and cultural diversity should be recognized and respected at the individual, group, and societal levels.
2. Ethnic and cultural diversity provides a basis for societal enrichment, cohesiveness, and survival.
3. Equality of opportunity should be afforded to members of all ethnic and cultural groups.
4. Ethnic and cultural identification should be optional for individuals in a democracy. (pp. 4–5)

A publication of the Center for Multicultural Education at the University of Washington, *Diversity within Unity: Essential Principles for Teaching and Learning in a Multicultural Society* (Banks, et al., 2001), will be helpful to school districts that are formulating a multicultural education policy statement. This publication also contains a useful checklist that will enable educators to determine the extent to which schools in their district reflect the 12 principles described in *Diversity within Unity*. A summary of the 12 principles—as well as information on how to order the publication or download it online—are found in Appendix A.

The School Staff

The school staff—including administrators, teachers, counselors, and the support staff—should reflect the racial and cultural diversity in U.S. society. The people students see working and interacting in the school environment teach them important lessons about the attitudes of adults toward racial, ethnic, and language diversity. Students need to see administrators, teachers, and counselors from different racial, ethnic, and language backgrounds in order for them to believe that U.S. society values and respects people from different ethnic, racial, cultural, and language groups. If most of the people students see in powerful and important positions in the school environment are from the dominant racial group, they will have a difficult time developing democratic racial attitudes, no matter how cogent are the words we speak about racial equality. Students' experiences speak much more powerfully than do the words they hear.

School districts should develop and implement an effective policy for the recruitment, hiring, and promotion of people from different racial and ethnic groups. Because most of the nation's teachers are White and female, school districts need to develop and implement innovative and experimental projects to increase the number of individuals of color who are entering the teaching profession (Darling-Hammond & Bransford, 2005; Ladson-Billings, 2001). A number of school districts have implemented or are participating in such innovative projects. Some of these projects consist of early identification programs in which promising students of color in high school are identified and given incentives for choosing teaching as a career.

Staff Attitudes and Expectations

School districts need to implement continuing staff development programs that help practicing educators to develop high expectations for low-income students and students of color and to better understand the cultural experiences of these students (Irvine, 2003). An increasing percentage of students in school today are from single-parent homes, have parents with special needs, and have cultural experiences that are dissimilar in significant ways from those of their teachers (García, 2005; Noguera, 2003a, b).

Many of these students have health, motivational, and educational needs that often challenge the most gifted and dedicated teachers. Yet many of these students are academically gifted and talented, although their gifts and talents are often not immediately evident and are not revealed by standardized mental ability tests (Fordham, 1996). Their academic gifts and talents are often obscured by skill deficits. Teachers must receive special training to develop the skills and sensitivities needed to perceive the hidden and underdeveloped talent and abilities of a significant number of students of color, language minority students, and low-income students (Ladson-Billings, 2001). Only when they are able to perceive the unrealized talent and potential of these students will teachers be able to increase their expectations for them (McNeil, 2000; Nieto, 2005; Valenzuela, 1999).

Gardner's (2006) theory of multiple intelligences can help teachers to reconceptualize the concept of intelligence and to develop a broader view of human ability. This broad view will enable them to see more intellectual strengths in culturally diverse and low-income students. Teachers should also use multiple culturally sensitive techniques to assess the complex cognitive and social skills of students who belong to diverse cultural, language, and social-class groups (Armour-Thomas & Gopaul-McNicol, 1998).

Creating successful experiences for students of color will enable them to develop a high self-concept of academic ability as well as enable their teachers to increase their academic expectations for them (Brookover et al., 1979; Brookover & Erickson, 1969). Student behavior and teacher expectations are related in an interactive way. The more teachers expect from students academically, the more they are likely to achieve; the more academically successful students are, the higher teacher expectations are likely to be for them (Green, 2000).

The Curriculum

The school curriculum should be reformed so that students will view concepts, events, issues, and problems from different ethnic perspectives and points of view (Banks, 2006c). Reconceptualizing the curriculum and making ethnic content an integral part of a transformed curriculum should be distinguished from merely adding ethnic content to the curriculum. Ethnic content can be added to the curriculum without transforming it or changing its basic assumptions, perspectives, and goals.

Content about Native Americans can be added to a Eurocentric curriculum that teaches students that Columbus discovered America. In such a curriculum, the students will read about Columbus's view of the Native Americans when he "discovered" them. In a transformed curriculum in which content about Native Americans is an integral part, the interaction of Columbus and Native Americans would not be conceptualized as Columbus "discovering" Native Americans (Bigelow & Peterson, 1998; Zinn, 2001). Rather, students would read about the culture of the Arawak Indians (also called Tainos) as it existed in the late 1400s (Olsen, 1974; Rouse, 1992), the journey of Columbus, and the meeting of the aboriginal American and European cultures in the Caribbean in 1492 (Josephy, 1992).

"Discovery" is not an accurate way to conceptualize and view the interaction of Columbus and the Arawaks unless this interaction is viewed exclusively from the point of view of Columbus and other Europeans. "The Meeting of Two Old World Cultures" is a more appropriate way to describe the Arawak–Columbus encounter. It is imperative that the encounter be viewed from the perspectives of the Arawaks or Tainos (Golden et al., 1991; Ponce de Leon, 1992; Stannard, 1992), in addition to that of Columbus and the Europeans (Morison, 1974). Excellent materials are available that teachers can use to teach diverse views of the Arawak-Columbus encounter. These materials include the special issue of the *National Geographic* (1991) on "America Before Columbus;" *Morning Girl*, a story by Michael Dorris (1992) about a 12-year-old Taino who lives on a Bahamian island in 1492; *Rethinking Columbus: The Next 500 Years* by Bigelow and Peterson (1998), and "Columbus and Western Civilization," an informative and powerful essay by Howard Zinn (2001) in *Howard Zinn on History*, a collection of his essays.

The multicultural curriculum not only helps students to view issues and problems from diverse ethnic perspectives and points of view, it is also *conceptual, interdisciplinary,* and *decision-making* focused (see Chapter 6). It helps students to make decisions on important issues and to take effective personal and civic action (Banks, 2006c).

The multicultural curriculum is a dynamic process. It is not possible to create a multicultural curriculum, hand it to teachers, and claim that a multicultural curriculum exists in the district. The teacher's role in its implementation is an integral part of a multicultural curriculum. Teachers mediate the curriculum with their values, perspectives, and teaching styles. Although multicultural materials are essential for implementing a multicultural curriculum, they are ineffective when used by teachers who lack a knowledge base in multicultural education or who do not have positive and clarified attitudes toward a range of racial, ethnic, language, and cultural groups. A well-designed, continuing staff development program is essential for the development and implementation of an effective multicultural curriculum (Ladson-Billings, 2001).

An effective preservice teacher education program is also essential for the successful implementation of multicultural education in the schools. School districts should demand that teacher education institutions have a strong multicultural education component in their programs as a condition for the employment of their graduates. The National Council for the Accreditation of Teacher Education has taken a leadership role in multicultural education by requiring its members to include multicultural education outcomes in their teacher education programs (NCATE, 1997, 2006). Most teacher education institutions in the United States are members of the National Council for the Accreditation of Teacher Education.

Parent Participation

Because of the enormity of the problems faced by schools today, it is not likely that the school can succeed in its major missions—helping students to attain academic skills and to become effective citizens of a democratic society—unless it can solicit the support of parents and the public-at-large (Comer, 2004; Hidalgo et al., 2004). However, soliciting the support of parents is a tremendous challenge for schools in today's society. Increasingly within the United States both parents work outside the home. Few families in the United States now conform to the standard-model family of past decades—a working father, mother at home, and two or more school-age children. According to the National Association of Child Care Resource and Referral Agencies (NACCRRA), 62 percent of mothers with children under five are now in the workforce (NACCRRA, 2006).

Other institutions are increasingly taking on functions that were in the past the primary responsibility of families. Because of the tremendous changes within U.S. society, we need to rethink the idea of parent involvement and reconceptualize ways in which parents can support the school, given the other demands now being made on their time (Comer, 2004). Asking a parent to provide a place for his or her child to study, to monitor the child's TV watching, and to restrict it to one hour per day may be a limited involvement, but it may be the only kind of parent involvement that the school can realistically expect from many parents who care deeply about their children's education.

Educators should be careful not to equate noninvolvement in traditional ways in school as lack of parent interest or lack of participation. Also, many parents are reluctant to get involved with schools because they lack a sense of empowerment and believe that their opinion will not matter anyway. Other parents are reluctant to become involved with schools because of their painful memories of their own school days. School districts should conceptualize and implement a program for involving parents in school that is consistent with the changing characteristics of families, parents, and society (C. A. M. Banks, 2007).

Teaching Strategies

The multicultural curriculum should be implemented with teaching strategies that are involving, interactive, personalized, and cooperative. The teacher should listen to and legitimize the voices of students from different racial, cultural, language, and gender groups. Multicultural content is inherently emotive, personal, conflictual, and interactive. Consequently, it is essential that students be given ample opportunities to express their feelings and emotions, to interact with their peers and classmates, and to express rage or pride when multicultural issues are discussed.

Didactic, teacher-centered instruction has serious disadvantages when teaching any kind of content. However, it is especially inappropriate when teaching multicultural content, an area in which diversity is valued and different perspectives are an integral part of the content. Students must be taught the skills needed to talk about race in civil, meaningful, and thoughtful ways. Conflict resolution and intergroup dialogue (Nagda, 2006) are skills that can be taught to students.

Teaching Materials

School districts need to develop and implement a policy for selecting teaching materials that describe the historical and contemporary experiences of various ethnic, language, and cultural groups and that present issues, problems, and concepts from the perspectives of these groups. It is not sufficient for textbooks and other teaching materials merely to include content about various ethnic, language, and cultural groups. The content about ethnic and cultural groups should be an integral part of the textbook or presentation and not an add-on or appendage. It is not un-common for content about people of color and women to be added to a textbook in a special section, as a special feature, or with photographs.

When ethnic content is placed in teaching materials primarily as add-ons or appendages, the text or presentation has not been reconcep-tualized or reformed in a way that will allow students to rethink the mainstream American metanarrative, to challenge their personal as-sumptions, or to develop new perspectives and insights on U.S. history and culture. If ethnic content is added to teaching materials and viewed from an Anglocentric perspective and point of view—which often hap-pens—then ethnic stereotypes and misconceptions held by students are likely to be reinforced rather than reduced. How ethnic content is inte-grated into textbooks and other teaching materials is as important as, if not more important than, whether it is included.

Monitoring

The successful implementation and improvement of a multicultural edu-cation program within a school or district require an effective monitoring plan. Ways must be developed to determine (1) whether the multicultural education goals established by the board of education are being attained, (2) steps that need to be taken to close the gap between the goals and ac-tual program implementation, and (3) incentives that are needed to mo-tivate people in the district to participate in the efforts being undertaken to attain the district's multicultural education goals and objectives.

An effective monitoring program may include (1) classroom visita-tions to determine the extent to which the content and strategies used by teachers are consistent with the cultural and language characteristics of students; (2) examination of standardized test scores disaggregated by race, social class, and language groups; and (3) examination of the per-centage of students of color who are suspended, who drop out, and who are classified as mentally retarded and gifted.

The monitoring program should not focus on specific individuals, such as teachers and principals, but should be systemic and focus on the total school as a unit. A systemic approach to monitoring will weaken re-sistance to a comprehensive monitoring program as well as reinforce the idea that multicultural education is a shared responsibility of the school and that everyone within the school building has a stake in its successful implementation, including the principal and teachers, as well as other members of the professional and support staffs, such as the secretary, the custodian, and the bus driver.

An effective and well-conceptualized monitoring program will provide the feedback needed to determine whether the benchmarks described in this chapter are being realized in your school, and the steps that need to be taken to ensure the ongoing improvement of its multicultural climate. The Multicultural Education Evaluation Checklist in Appendix C is designed to help you assess the environment of your school and to plan and implement action to make it more consistent with the multicultural realities of the United States and the world.

Closing the Achievement Gap

A major goal of multicultural education is to create equal educational opportunities for students from different racial, ethnic, language, and social-class groups (see Chapter 7). The gaps in academic achievement, drop-out, and graduation rates for students from different racial and income groups are enormous in most school districts. Each school district needs to determine the gaps in academic achievement, drop-out rates, and graduation rates for students from different racial, language, and income groups. The No Child Left Behind Act—enacted by Congress in 2001 and signed by President George W. Bush in 2002—requires school districts to disaggregate achievement data by income, race, ethnicity, disability, and limited English proficiency. Each district also needs to develop a comprehensive and well-conceptualized plan for closing these gaps.

Special attention should also be given to the proportion of students of color that is expelled or suspended from school and the percentage that is enrolled in special education and in classes for gifted students (Ford, 2007). In most school districts, students of color—especially males—are overrepresented among the students who are suspended from school and in classes for the mentally retarded (Reschly, 1988). However, these students are usually underrepresented in classes for gifted students (Ford, 1996).

A goal of each school district should be to have students from different racial, language, and social-class groups represented in special education and in gifted classes roughly equal to their percentage in their district's population. This means that the percentage of students of color in special education would be reduced and their percentage in classes for gifted students would increase in most school districts.

A

Essential Principles for Teaching and Learning in a Multicultural Society

What do we know about education and diversity and how do we know it? This two-part question guided the Multicultural Education Consensus Panel that was sponsored by the Center for Multicultural Education at the University of Washington and the Common Destiny Alliance at the University of Maryland. The findings of the Consensus Panel are the product of a four-year project during which the panel reviewed and synthesized research related to diversity. The panel's work was supported by a grant from the Carnegie Corporation of New York. The panel members are specialists in race relations and multicultural education. An interdisciplinary group, it was made up of two psychologists, a political scientist, a sociologist, and four multicultural education specialists. The panel was modeled after the consensus panels that develop and write reports for the National Research Council of the National Academy of Sciences. In National Research Council panels, an expert group decides, based on research and practice, what is known about a particular problem and the most effective actions that can be taken to solve it.

The findings of the Multicultural Education Consensus Panel, which are called essential principles, describe ways in which educational policy

From J. A. Banks, P. Cookson, G. Gay, W. D. Hawley, J. J. Irvine, S. Nieto, J. Ward Schofield, & W. G. Stephan (2001), *Diversity within Unity: Essential Principles for Teaching and Learning in a Multicultural Society*. Seattle: Center for Multicultural Education, University of Washington. Reprinted with permission.

Information for ordering this publication and for downloading it can be obtained on the center's website: http://depts.washington.edu/centerme/home.htm.

121

and practice related to diversity can be improved. These principles are derived from research and practice. They are designed to help educational practitioners in all types of schools increase student academic achievement and improve intergroup skills. Another aim is to help schools successfully meet the challenges of and benefit from the diversity that characterizes the United States and its schools. A summary of the 12 essential principles identified by the Consensus Panel follow. Readers can examine *Diversity within Unity,* the publication in which the design principles are described, online as well as order the publication from the Center for Multicultural Education, University of Washington, Seattle. On-line and ordering information is at the bottom of page 121.

Teacher Learning

Principle 1: Professional development programs should help teachers understand the complex characteristics of ethnic groups within U.S. society and the ways in which race, ethnicity, language, and social class interact to influence student behavior.

Student Learning

Principle 2: Schools should ensure that all students have equitable opportunities to learn and to meet high standards.

Principle 3: The curriculum should help students understand that knowledge is socially constructed and reflects researchers' personal experiences as well as the social, political, and economic contexts in which they live and work.

Principle 4: Schools should provide all students with opportunities to participate in extra- and cocurricular activities that develop knowledge, skills, and attitudes that increase academic achievement and foster positive interracial relationships.

Intergroup Relations

Principle 5: Schools should create or make salient superordinate crosscutting group memberships in order to improve intergroup relations.

Principle 6: Students should learn about stereotyping and other related biases that have negative effects on racial and ethnic relations.

Principle 7: Students should learn about the values shared by virtually all cultural groups (e.g., justice, equality, freedom, peace, compassion, and charity).

Principle 8: Teachers should help students acquire the social skills needed to interact effectively with students from other racial, ethnic, cultural, and language groups.

Principle 9: Schools should provide opportunities for students from different racial, ethnic, cultural, and language groups to interact socially under conditions designed to reduce fear and anxiety.

School Governance, Organization, and Equity

Principle 10: A school's organizational strategies should ensure that decision making is widely shared and that members of the school community learn collaborative skills and dispositions in order to create a caring environment for students.

Principle 11: Leaders should develop strategies that ensure that all public schools, regardless of their locations, are funded equitably.

Assessment

Principle 12: Teachers should use multiple culturally sensitive techniques to assess complex cognitive and social skills.

B

Checklist for Evaluating Informational Materials

Criteria Questions	Rating Hardly at all ↔ Extensively					
1. Includes a range of racial, ethnic, and cultural groups that reflects the diversity within U.S. life and society.						
2. Describes the wide range of diversity that exists within racial, ethnic, and cultural groups (for example, social class, regional, ideology, and language diversity within ethnic groups).						
3. Describes the roles, experiences, challenges, and contributions of women within various racial and ethnic groups.						
4. Helps students to view American history and society from the perspectives of women within various racial and ethnic groups, such as African American women who played major roles in the Civil Rights movement but who are often not given much visibility compared to men in the movement (e.g., Ella Baker, Jo Ann Gipson Robinson, and Fannie Lou Hammer).						

Criteria Questions	Rating Hardly at all ↔ Extensively					
5. Describes the range of dialects and languages within U.S. society, the problems of language minority groups, and the contributions that diverse languages make to U.S. society.						
6. Integrates the histories and experiences of racial and ethnic groups into the mainstream story of the development of America rather than isolating them into special sections, boxes, and features.						
7. Challenges the concepts of American exceptionalism and manifest destiny and helps students to develop new views of the development of the United States.						
8. Helps students to view the historical development of the United States from the perspectives of groups that have been victimized in American history (such as Native Americans, Mexican Americans, African Americans, and lower socioeconomic groups) and from the perspectives of groups that have been advantaged in America, such as Anglo-Saxon Protestants and higher-income groups.						
9. Uses primary resources to document and describe the experiences of racial, ethnic, and cultural groups in the United States.						
10. Helps students to understand the powerful role of social class in U.S. society and the extent to which class is still a significant factor in determining the life chances of U.S. citizens.						
11. Helps students to understand the extent to which *acculturation* within U.S. society is a two-way process and the ways in which majority groups have incorporated (and sometimes appropriated) aspects of the cultures of ethnic groups of color and the extent to which ethnic groups of color have adapted and incorporated mainstream culture into their ways of life.						

Criteria Questions	Rating Hardly at all ↔ Extensively					
12. Helps students to understand the extent to which the American dream of equality for all citizens is still incomplete and the role that students need to play to help close the gap between American democratic ideals and realities.						
13. The mathematics and science materials help students to understand the ways in which the assumptions, perspectives, and problems within these fields are often culturally based and influenced.						
14. The mathematics and science materials describe the ways in which these disciplines influence the knowledge that is constructed about racial, ethnic, cultural, and gender groups.						
15. The mathematics and science materials help students to understand the ways in which people from a variety of cultures and groups have contributed to the development of scientific and mathematical knowledge.						
16. Acquaints students with key concepts that are essential for understanding the history and cultures of racial, ethnic, and cultural groups in the United States, such as prejudice, discrimination, institutionalized racism, institutionalized sexism, and social-class stratification.						
17. Acquaints students with key historical and cultural events that are essential for understanding the experiences of racial and ethnic groups in the United States, such as the Harlem Renaissance, the Middle Passage, the internment of Japanese Americans, the Treaty of Guadalupe Hidalgo, and the Trail of Tears.						

A Multicultural Education Evaluation Checklist

Criteria Questions	Rating Hardly at all ↔ Extensively		
1. Does school policy reflect the ethnic, cultural, and gender diversity in U.S. society?			
2. Is the total school culture (including the hidden curriculum) multiethnic and multicultural?			
3. Do the learning styles favored by the school reflect the learning styles of the students?			
4. Does the school reflect and sanction the range of languages and dialects spoken by the students and within the larger society?			
5. Does the school involve parents from diverse ethnic and cultural groups in school activities, programs, and planning?			

Criteria Questions	Rating Hardly at all ↔ Extensively		
6. Does the counseling program of the school reflect the ethnic diversity in U.S. society?			
7. Are the testing procedures used by the school multicultural and ethnically fair?			
8. Are instructional materials examined for ethnic, cultural, and gender bias?			
9. Are the formalized curriculum and course of study multiethnic and multicultural? Do they help students to view events, situations, and concepts from diverse ethnic and cultural perspectives and points of view?			
10. Do the teaching styles and motivational systems in the school reflect the ethnic and cultural diversity of the student body?			
11. Are the attitudes, perceptions, beliefs, and behavior of the total staff ethnically and racially sensitive?			
12. Does the school have systematic, comprehensive, mandatory, and continuing multicultural staff development programs?			
13. Is the school staff (administrative, instructional, counseling, and supportive) multiethnic and multicultural?			
14. Is the total atmosphere of the school positively responsive to racial, ethnic, cultural, and language differences?			
15. Do school assemblies and holidays reflect the ethnic and cultural diversity in U.S. society?			

Criteria Questions	Rating Hardly at all ↔ Extensively		
16. Does the school lunch program prepare meals that reflect the range of ethnic foods eaten in the United States?			
17. Do the bulletin boards, physical education program, music, and other displays and activities in the school reflect ethnic and cultural diversity?			

Source: Adapted from J. A. Banks (1981), "Multiethnic Education and School Reform." In L. V. Edinger, P. L. Houts, & D. V. Meyer (Eds.), *Education in the 80s: Curricular Challenges* (pp. 112–123). Washington, DC: National Education Association.

A Multicultural Education Basic Library

Books

Banks, J. A. (Ed.). (1996–continuing). *Multicultural education series.* A series of books—written by authors from diverse racial and ethnic groups—that focus on research, theory, and practice in multicultural education. Teachers College Press, Columbia University, 1234 Amsterdam Avenue, New York, NY 10027. Authors include Gary Howard, Sonia Nieto, Pedro Noguera, Guadalupe Valdés, Geneva Gay, Carol Lee, and Linda Darling-Hammond. Website: www.teacherscollegepress.com

Banks, J. A. (2003). *Teaching strategies for ethnic studies* (6th ed.). Boston: Allyn and Bacon.

Banks, J. A., & Banks, C. A. M. (Eds.). (2004). *Handbook of research on multicultural education* (2nd ed.). San Francisco: Jossey-Bass.

Banks, J. A., & Banks, C. A. M. (Eds.). (2007). *Multicultural education: Issues and perspectives* (6th ed.). New York: Wiley.

Banks, J. A., Banks, C. A. M., Cortes, C. E., Merryfield, M. M., Moodley, K. A., Murphy-Shigematsu, S., Osler, A., Park, C., & Parker, W. C. (2005). *Democracy and diversity: Principles and concepts for educating citizens in a global age.* Seattle: University of Washington, Center for Multicultural Education.

Banks, J. A., Cookson, P., Gay, G., Hawley, W. D., Irvine, J. J., Nieto, S., Schofield, J. W., & Stephan, W. G. (2001). *Diversity within unity: Essential principles for teaching and learning in a multicultural society.* Seattle: University of Washington, Center for Multicultural Education.

Gay, G. (2000). *Culturally responsive teaching: Theory, research and practice.* New York: Teachers College Press.

Grant, C. A., & Ladson-Billings, G. (Eds.). (1997). *Dictionary of multicultural education*. Phoenix: The Oryx Press.

Howard, G. (2006). *We can't teach what we don't know: White teachers, multiracial schools* (2nd ed.). New York: Teachers College Press.

Muse, D. (Ed.). (1997). *The New Press guide to multicultural resources for young readers*. New York: New Press.

Nieto, S. (1999). *The light in their eyes: Creating multicultural learning communities*. New York: Teachers College Press.

Stephan, W. G., & Vogt, W. P. (Eds.). (2004). *Education programs for improving intergroup relations: Theory, research, and practice*. New York: Teachers College Press.

Takaki, R. (1993). *A different mirror: A history of multicultural America*. Boston: Little, Brown.

Journals and Magazines

Intercultural Education, the official journal of the International Association for Intercultural Education (IAIE). This quarterly journal includes articles on intercultural education from around the world. It is edited in The Netherlands and is published quarterly by Taylor and Francis.

Multicultural Education, a quarterly journal that includes articles, book reviews, and other features. Published by Gaddo Gap Press, 3145 Geary Boulevard, PMB 275, San Francisco, CA 94118. Website: www.caddogap.com/.

Multicultural Perspectives, an official journal of the National Association for Multicultural Education. Published four times a year by Lawrence Erlbaum Associates, Inc., 10 Industrial Avenue, Mahwah, NJ 07430.

Multicultural Review, published quarterly by The Goldman Group Inc., 14497 North Dale Mabry Hwy, Suite 205-N, Tampa, FL 33618; telephone 813-264-2772; fax 813-264-2343.

A comprehensive source of reviews of books for children and youth that deal with racial, ethnic, cultural, and religious groups.

Race Equality Teaching. A quarterly journal published in the United Kingdom. Its main audience is educational practitioners. Published by Trentham Books, Westview House, 734 London Road, Stoke-on-Trent, ST4 5NP, United Kingdom; telephone +44 (0) 1782 745567; fax +44 (0) 1782 745553. Website: www.trenthambooks.co.uk.

Race Ethnicity and Education. This is a scholarly journal that is edited by Professor David Gillborn at the University of London, Institute of Education. However, it publishes articles and book reviews from around the world. It is published by Taylor and Francis.

Rethinking Schools. A quarterly magazine edited by teachers for teachers in Milwaukee. Rethinking Schools also publishes excellent books for teachers. 101

East Keefe Avenue, Milwaukee, WI 53212. Website: www.rethinkingschools. org.

Teaching Tolerance, a magazine published twice a year by Teaching Tolerance, a division of the Southern Poverty Law Center, 400 Washington Avenue, Montgomery, AL 36104. Distributed free to school and university educators. Teaching Tolerance also produces and distributes excellent videotapes that can be used in schools and for teacher education courses. Website: http://www.splcenter.org/teachingtolerance.

Catalogs

Anti-Defamation League Resources for Classroom and Community. An excellent and comprehensive annually published catalog of books, videotapes, posters, and other materials for use in the multicultural classroom school. Copies of *Resources* are available upon request. Fill out the on-line order form (http:// www.adl.org/catalog/default.asp) or call 800-343-5540 for more information. The Anti-Defamation League, founded in 1913, is the world's leading organization fighting anti-Semitism through programs and services that counteract hatred, prejudice, and bigotry. Mailing address: Anti-Defamation League, 823 United Nations Plaza, New York, NY 10017.

Arte Publico Press Catalog. Arte Publico Press is the oldest and largest publisher of U.S. Hispanic literature. A catalog of fiction, poetry, drama, literary criticism, and art by leading figures in Mexican American, Puerto Rican, Cuban, and U.S. Hispanic literature, it includes books for children and young people. University of Houston, Houston, TX 77204-2090. Published annually, with supplements during the year. Website: http://www.arte.uh.edu/.

Lee & Low Books Catalog. Lee & Low Books publishes multicultural literature for children. 95 Madison Avenue, New York, NY 10016. Published annually. Website: /www.leeandlow.com/.

Social Studies School Services Catalog. This catalog includes a section that describes teaching materials about ethnic groups in the United States as well as about global studies. A comprehensive collection of books, posters, videotapes, and other materials for the diverse classroom. Social Studies School Services, Culver City, California. Website: http://www.socialstudies.com.

Teaching for Change. This catalog features books and resources on immigration, war and the Middle East, early childhood education, and civil rights. P.O. Box 73038, Washington, DC 20056-3038. Website: www.teachingforchange.org.

Glossary

Afrocentric Explanations, cultural characteristics, teaching materials, and other factors related to the heritages, histories, and cultures of people of African descent who live in the United States and in other parts of the world. The U.S. Census indicates that there were approximately 37.5 million African Americans living in the United States in 2004.

Anglocentric Explanations, cultural characteristics, teaching materials, and other factors related to the heritages, histories, and cultures of Whites of British descent in the United States.

Canon A standard or criterion used to define, select, and evaluate knowledge in the school and university curriculum within a nation. The list of book-length works or readings selected using the standard is also described as the canon. Historically in the United States, the canon that has dominated the curriculum has been Eurocentric and male-oriented.

Culture The ideations, symbols, behaviors, values, and beliefs that are shared by a human group. Culture may also be defined as the symbols, institutions, or other components of human societies that are created by human groups to meet their survival needs.

Ethnic group A group that shares a common history, a sense of peoplehood and identity, values, behavioral characteristics, and a communication system. The members of an ethnic group usually view their group as distinct and separate from other cultural groups within a society. Ethnic groups within the United States include Anglo Americans, Irish Americans, Polish Americans, and German Americans.

Ethnic minority group   An ethnic group that has unique behavioral and/or racial characteristics that enable other groups to easily identify its members. These groups are often a numerical minority within the nation-state and the victims of institutionalized discrimination. Jewish Americans are an example of an ethnic group differentiated on the basis of cultural and religious characteristics. African Americans, Mexican Americans, and Japanese Americans are differentiated on the basis of both biological and cultural characteristics.

The term *ethnic minority group* is being used increasingly less within U.S. educational communities because of the nation's changing racial, ethnic, and language characteristics. In these six states, students of color exceed the number of White students in the public schools: California, Hawaii, Louisiana, Mississippi, New Mexico, and Texas. The U.S. Census (2000) projects that by the year 2050 Whites and people of color will each make up about 50 percent of the U.S. population. Consequently, the United States will be made up of groups of minorities. The term *people of color* is increasingly replacing ethnic minority group in educational discourse in the United States.

Ethnic-specific programs   Curricula and educational policies that focus on one designated ethnic group, such as Anglo Americans, Latino Americans, or Asian Americans, rather than on a range of ethnic and cultural groups.

Ethnic studies   The scientific and humanistic study of the histories, cultures, and experiences of ethnic groups within the United States and in other societies.

Eurocentric explanations   Cultural characteristics, teaching materials, and other factors related to the heritages, histories, and cultures of people of European descent who live in the United States and in other nations.

Global education   The study of the cultures, institutions, and interconnectedness of nations outside of the United States. Global education is often confused with multicultural education, which deals with educational issues in the United States or within another nation. Global education deals with issues, problems, and developments outside of the United States or outside another nation.

Knowledge construction   The process that helps students understand how social, behavioral, and natural scientists create knowledge, and how their implicit cultural assumptions, frames of reference, perspectives, cultural contexts, and biases influence the knowledge they construct. Knowledge construction teaching strategies, which are constructivist, involve students in activities that enable them to create their own interpretations of the past, present, and future.

Multicultural education   An educational reform movement whose major goal is to restructure curricula and educational institutions so that students from diverse social-class, racial, and ethnic groups—as well as both gender groups—will experience equal educational opportunities. Multicultural education consists of three major components: (1) an educational reform movement whose aim is to create equal educational opportunities for all students; (2) an ideology whose aim is to actualize American democratic ideals, such as equality, justice, and human rights; and (3) a process that never ends because there will always be a discrepancy between democratic ideals and school and societal practices.

Multiculturalists   A group of theorists, researchers, and educators who believe that the curricula within the nation's schools, colleges, and universities should be reformed so that they reflect the experiences and perspectives of the diverse cultures and groups in U.S. society.

Multiethnic education   An educational reform movement designed to restructure educational institutions so that students from diverse ethnic groups, such as Asian Americans, Native Americans, and Latinos, will experience equal educational opportunities. This term was used frequently in the 1970s but is rarely used in educational discourse today.

Paradigm   An interrelated set of facts, concepts, generalizations, and theories that attempt to explain human behavior or a social phenomenon and that imply policy and action. A paradigm, which is also a set of explanations, has specific goals, assumptions, and values that can be described. Paradigms compete with one another in the arena of ideas and educational policy. Explanations such as at-risk students, culturally deprived students, and culturally different students are paradigms.

Paradigm shift   The process that occurs when an individual accepts and internalizes an explanation or theory to explain a phenomenon or event that differs substantially from the one that he or she previously had internalized. An example occurs when an individual who previously believed that Columbus discovered America now views the Columbus-Arawak encounter as the meeting of two old-world cultures.

People of color   A term used to refer to racial groups in the United States that have historically experienced institutionalized discrimination and racism because of their physical characteristics. These groups include African Americans, Asian Americans, Latinos, Native Americans, and Native Hawaiians.

Powerful ideas   Key concepts or themes—such as culture, socialization, power, and discrimination—that are used to organize lessons, units, and courses. In conceptual teaching, instruction focuses on helping students to see relationships and to derive principles and generalizations.

Transformative curriculum   A curriculum that challenges the basic assumptions and implicit values of the Eurocentric, male-dominated curriculum institutionalized in U.S. schools, colleges, and universities. It helps students to view concepts, events, and situations from diverse racial, ethnic, gender, and social-class perspectives. The transformative curriculum also helps students to construct their own interpretations of the past, present, and future.

Western traditionalists   Social scientists, historians, and other scholars who argue that the European Western tradition should be at the center of the curriculum in U.S. schools, colleges, and universities because of the cogent influence that Western ideas and ideals have had on the development of the United States and the world.

References

Aboud, F. E., & Doyle, A. B. (1996). Does talk foster prejudice or tolerance in children? *Canadian Journal of Behavioural Science, 28*(3), 161–171.

Addison-Wesley. (1993). *Multiculturalism in mathematics, science, and technology: Readings and activities.* Menlo Park, CA: Addison-Wesley.

Alba, R. (1990). *Ethnic identity: The transformation of White America.* New Haven, CT: Yale University Press.

Alba, R., & Nee, V. (2003). *Remaking the American mainstream: Assimilation and contemporary immigration.* Cambridge, MA: Harvard University Press.

Alim, H. S., & Baugh, J. (Eds.). (2007). *Talkin Black talk: Language, education, and social change.* New York: Teachers College Press.

Allen, P. G. (1986). *The sacred hoop: Recovering the feminine in American Indian traditions.* Boston: Beacon Press.

Allport, G. W. (1954). *The nature of prejudice.* Reading, MA: Addison-Wesley.

Amrein, A. L., & Berliner, D. C. (2002). High-stakes testing, uncertainty, and student learning. *Education Policy Analysis Archives, 10*(18). Retrieved February 14, 2003, from http://epaa.asu.edu/epaa/v10n18/.

Anderson, B. (1991). *Imagined communities: Reflections on the origin and spread of nationalism.* New York: Verso.

Anyon, J. (2005). *Radical possibilities: Public policy, urban education, and a new social movement.* New York: Routledge.

Anzaldua, G. (1999). *Borderlands: The new Mestiza.* San Francisco: Spinsters/Aunt Lute.

Appiah, K. A. (2006). *Cosmopolitanism: Ethnics in a world of strangers.* New York: Norton.

Appiah, K. A., & Gates, H. L., Jr. (Eds.). (2005). *Africana: The encyclopedia of the African and African American experience* (5 vols.). Oxford & New York: Oxford University Press.

Applebee, A. N. (1993). *Literature in the secondary school: Studies of curriculum and instruction.* Urbana, IL: National Council of Teachers of English.

Armitage, S. (1987). Through women's eyes: A new view of the west. In S. Armitage & E. Jameson (Eds.), *The women's west* (pp. 9–18). Norman: University of Oklahoma Press.

Armour-Thomas, E., & Gopaul-McNicol, S. (1998). *Assessing intelligence: Applying a bio-cultural model.* Thousand Oaks, CA: Sage.

Aronson, E., & Bridgeman, D. (1979). Jigsaw groups and the desegregated classroom: In pursuit of common goals. *Personality and Social Psychology Bulletin, 5,* 438–446.

Aronson, E., & Gonzalez, A. (1988). Desegregation, jigsaw, and the Mexican-American experience. In P. A. Katz & D. A. Taylor (Eds.), *Eliminating racism: Profiles in controversy* (pp. 301–314). New York: Plenum Press.

Artiles, A. J., & Zamora-Duran, G. (Eds.). (1997). *Reducing disproportionate representation of culturally diverse students in special and gifted education.* Reston, VA: Council for Exceptional Children.

Asante, M. (1998). *The Afrocentric idea* (rev. & exp. ed.). Philadelphia: Temple University Press.

Asante, M. K., & Mazama, A. (Eds.). (2005). *Encyclopedia of Black studies.* Thousand Oaks, CA: Sage.

Ascher, M. (1991). *Ethnomathematics: A multicultural view of mathematical ideas.* Pacific Grove, CA: Brooks/Cole.

Ascher, M., & Ascher, R. (1981). *The code of the Quipu: A study in media, mathematics and culture.* Ann Arbor: University of Michigan Press.

Au, K. (2006). *Multicultural issues and literacy achievement.* Mahwah, NJ: Erlbaum.

Au, K. H. (1979). Using the experience-text-relationship method with minority children. *Reading Teacher, 32*(6), 677, 679.

Au, K. H., & Kawakami, A. J. (1985). Research currents: Talk story and learning to read. *Language Arts, 62*(4), 406–411.

August, D., & Shanahan, T. (Eds.). (2006). *Developing literacy in second-language learners: Report of the National Literacy Panel on Language-Minority Children and Youth.* Mahwah, NJ: Erlbaum.

Back, L., & Solomos, J. (Eds.). (2000). *Theories of race and racism.* London & New York: Routledge.

Baldwin, J. (1985). A talk to teachers. In *The price of the ticket: Collected nonfiction, 1948–1985* (pp. 325–332). New York: St. Martin's.

Banks, C. A. M. (2005). *Improving multicultural education: Lessons from the intergroup education movement.* New York: Teachers College Press.

Banks, C. A. M. (2007). Families and teachers working together for school improvement. In J. A. Banks & C. A. M. Banks (Eds.), *Multicultural education: Issues and perspectives* (6th ed., pp. 445–465). Hoboken, NJ: Wiley.

Banks, J. A. (1993). Multicultural education for young children: Racial and ethnic attitudes and their modification. In B. Spodek (Ed.), *Handbook of research on the education of young children* (pp. 236–250). New York: Macmillan.

Banks, J. A. (Ed.). (1996a). *Multicultural education, transformative knowledge, and action: Historical and contemporary perspectives.* New York: Teachers College Press.

Banks, J. A. (1996b). The canon debate, knowledge construction, and multicultural education. In J. A. Banks (Ed.), *Multicultural education, transformative knowledge, and action* (pp. 3–29). New York: Teachers College Press.

Banks, J. A. (1997). *Educating citizens in a multicultural society.* New York: Teachers College Press.

Banks, J. A. (2001). Multicultural education: Its effects on students' racial and gender role attitudes. In J. A. Banks & C. A. M. Banks (Eds.), *Handbook of research on multicultural education* (pp. 617–627). San Francisco: Jossey-Bass.

Banks, J. A. (2002). Teaching for diversity and unity in a democratic multicultural society. In W. C. Parker (Ed.), *Education for democracy: Contexts, curricula, assessments* (pp. 131–150). Greenwich, CT: Information Age Publishing.

Banks, J. A. (2003). *Teaching strategies for ethnic studies* (7th ed.). Boston: Allyn and Bacon.

Banks, J. A. (Ed.). (2004a). *Diversity and citizenship education: Global perspectives.* San Francisco: Jossey-Bass.

Banks, J. A. (2004b). Introduction: Democratic citizenship education in multicultural societies. In J. A. Banks (Ed.), *Diversity and citizenship education: Global perspectives* (pp. 3–15). San Francisco: Jossey-Bass.

Banks, J. A. (2004c). Multicultural education: Historical development, dimensions, and practice. In J. A. Banks & C. A. M. Banks (Eds.), *Handbook of research on multicultural education* (2nd ed., pp. 3–29). San Francisco: Jossey-Bass.

Banks, J. A. (2006a). Commentary: Improving race relations in schools: From theory and research to practice. *Journal of Social Issues, 62*(3), 607–614.

Banks, J. A. (2006b). *Cultural diversity and education: Foundations, curriculum, and teaching* (5th ed.). Boston: Allyn and Bacon.

Banks, J. A. (2006c). *Race, culture, and education: The selected works of James A. Banks.* London & New York: Routledge.

Banks, J. A. (2007). Approaches to multicultural curriculum reform. In J. A. Banks & C. A. M. Banks (Eds.), *Multicultural education: Issues and perspectives* (6th ed., pp. 247–269). Hoboken, NJ: Wiley.

Banks, J. A., & Banks, C. A. M. (Eds.). (2004). *Handbook of research on multicultural education* (2nd ed.). San Francisco: Jossey-Bass.

Banks, J. A., & Banks, C. A. M. (Eds.). (2007). *Multicultural education: Issues and perspectives* (6th ed., pp. 401–421). Hoboken, NJ: Wiley.

Banks, J. A., & Banks, C. A. M., with Clegg, A. A. (1999). *Teaching strategies for the social studies: Decision-making and citizen action* (5th ed.). New York: Longman.

Banks, J. A., Banks, C. A. M., Cortes, C. E., Merryfield, M. M., Moodley, K. A., Murphy-Shigematsu, S., Osler, A., Park, C., & Parker, W. C. (2005). *Democracy and diversity: Principles and concepts for educating citizens in a global age.* Seattle: University of Washington, Center for Multicultural Education.

Banks, J. A., Cookson, P., Gay, G., Hawley, W. D., Irvine, J. J., Nieto, S., Schofield, J. W., & Stephan, W. G. (2001). *Diversity within unity: Essential principles for teaching and learning in a multicultural society.* Seattle: University of Washington, Center for Multicultural Education.

Banks, J. A., Cortés, C. E., Gay, G., Garcia, R. L., & Ochoa, A. (1992). *Curriculum guidelines for multicultural education* (rev. ed.). Washington, DC: National Council for the Social Studies.

Banks, J. A., with Sebesta, S. L. (1982). *We Americans: Our history and people* (vols. 1 and 2). Boston: Allyn and Bacon.

Battle, M. (2006). *The Black church in America: African American Christian spirituality.* Malden, MA: Blackwell.

Bender, T. (2006). *A nation among nations: America's place in world history.* New York: Hill and Wang.

Benhabib, S. (2004). *The rights of others: Aliens, residents, and citizens.* New York: Cambridge University Press.

Bernal, M. (1987). *Black Athena: The Afroasiatic roots of classical civilization.* Volume 1: *The fabrication of ancient Greece, 1785–1985.* London: Free Association Books.

Bernal, M. (1991). *Black Athena: The Afroasiatic roots of classical civilization.* Volume 2: *The archaeological and documentary evidence.* New Brunswick, NJ: Rutgers University Press.

Bhatia, T. K., & Ritchie, W. C. (Eds.). (2004). *The handbook of bilingualism.* Malden, MA: Blackwell.

Bigelow, B., Harvey, B., Karp, S., & Miller, L. (2001). *Rethinking our classrooms: Teaching for equity and justice* (vol. 2). Milwaukee, WI: Rethinking Schools Press.

Bigelow, B., & Peterson, B. (1998). *Rethinking Columbus: The next 500 years.* Milwaukee: Rethinking Schools.

Bigelow, B., & Peterson, B. (Eds.). (2002). *Rethinking globalization: Teaching for justice in an unjust world.* Milwaukee, WI: Rethinking Schools Press.

Bloom, H. (1994). *The Western canon: The books and school of the ages.* New York: Harcourt.

Bogatz, G. A., & Ball, S. (1971). *The second year of Sesame Street: A continuing evaluation.* Princeton, NJ: Educational Testing Service.

Boykin, A. W. (2000). The talent development model of schooling: Placing students at promise for academic success. *Journal of Education for Students Placed at Risk, 5*(1 & 2), 3–25.

Boykin, A. W., & Slavin, R. (Eds.). (2000). CRESPAR Findings (1994–1999): In memory of John H. Hollifield, Jr. *Journal of Education for Students Placed at Risk, 5* (Special issue, 1 & 2), 3–208.

Branch, T. (2006). *At Canaan's edge: America in the King years, 1965–68.* New York: Simon & Schuster.

Brinton, C. (1962). *The anatomy of revolution.* New York: Vintage.

Brodkin, K. (1998). *How the Jews became White folks and what that says about race in America.* New Brunswick, NJ: Rutgers University Press.

Brookover, W., Beady, C., Flood, P., Schweitzer, J., & Wisenbaker, J. (1979). *School social systems and student achievement: Schools can make a difference.* New York: Praeger.

Brookover, W. B., & Erickson, E. L. (1969). *Society, schools, and learning.* Boston: Allyn and Bacon.

Bruner, J. S. (1960). *The process of education*. Cambridge, MA: Harvard University Press.

Bureau of Economic Analysis. (2006). Foreign direct investment in the United States. Retrieved August 23, 2006, from http://www.state.gov/r/pa/prs/ps/2006/63553.htm.

Burns, G. M. (1978). *Leadership*. New York: Harper & Row.

Byrnes, D. A., & Kiger, G. (1990). The effect of prejudice-reduction simulation on attitude change. *Journal of Applied Social Psychology, 20*(4), 341–356.

Cain, W. E. (Ed.). (1994). *Teaching the conflicts: Gerald Graff, curricular reform, and the culture wars*. New York: Garland.

Castles, S. (2004). Migration, citizenship, and education. In J. A. Banks (Ed.), *Diversity and citizenship education: Global perspectives* (pp. 17–48). San Francisco: Jossey-Bass.

Castles, S., & Davidson, A. (2000). *Citizenship and migration: Globalization and the politics of belonging*. New York: Routledge.

Cesari, J. (2004). *When Islam and democracy meet: Muslims in Europe and the United States*. New York: Pelgrave Macmillan.

Champagne, D. (1994). *Native America: Portrait of the peoples*. Detroit: Visible Ink.

Chavez, L. (1991). *Out of the barrio: Toward a new politics of Hispanic assimilation*. New York: Basic Books.

Ciullo, R., & Troiani, M. Y. (1988). Resolution of prejudice: Small group interaction and behavior of latency-age children. *Small Group Behavior, 19*(3), 386–394.

Clarke, J. H. (1990). African people on my mind. In A. G. Hilliard III, L. Payton-Stewart, & W. Obadele (Eds.), *Infusion of African and African American content in the school curriculum: Proceedings of the first national conference* (pp. 50–59). Morristown, NJ: Aaron Press.

Code, L. (1991). *What can she know? Feminist theory and the construction of knowledge*. Ithaca, NY: Cornell University Press.

Cohen, E. (1972). Interracial interaction disability. *Human Relations, 25*, 9–24.

Cohen, E. G. (1984a). Talking and working together: Status, interaction, and learning. In P. Peterson, L. C. Wilkinson, & M. Hallinan (Eds.), *The social context of instruction* (pp. 171–186). New York: Academic Press.

Cohen, E. G. (1984b). The desegregated school: Problems in status power and interethnic climate. In N. Miller & M. B. Brewer (Eds.), *Groups in contact: The psychology of desegregation* (pp. 77–96). New York: Academic Press.

Cohen, E. G. (1994). *Designing groupwork: Strategies for the heterogeneous classroom* (2nd ed.). New York: Teachers College Press.

Cohen, E. G., & Lotan, R. A. (1995). Producing equal-status interaction in the heterogeneous classroom. *American Educational Research Journal, 32*, 99–120.

Cohen, E., & Lotan, R. A. (Eds.). (1997). *Working for equity in heterogeneous classrooms*. New York: Teachers College Press.

Cohen, E. G., & Roper, S. S. (1972). Modification of interracial interaction disability: An application of status characteristic theory. *American Sociological Review, 37*, 643–657.

Collins, P. H. (2000). *Black feminist thought: Knowledge, consciousness, and the politics of empowerment* (2nd ed.). New York: Routledge.

Comer, J. P. (2004). *Leave no child behind: Preparing today's youth for tomorrow's world*. New Haven: Yale University Press.

Conchas, G. Q. (2006). *The color of success: Race and high-achieving urban youth*. New York: Teachers College Press.

Cose, E. (1993). *The rage of a privileged class*. New York: HarperCollins.

Cross, W. E., Jr. (1991). *Shades of black: Diversity in African-American identity*. Philadelphia: Temple University Press.

Darling-Hammond, L. (1997). *The right to learn: A blueprint for creating schools that work*. San Francisco: Jossey-Bass.

Darling-Hammond, L., & Bransford, J. (Eds.). (2005). *Preparing teachers for a changing world: What teachers should learn and be able to do*. San Francisco: Jossey-Bass.

Davis, F. J. (1991). *Who is Black? One nation's definition*. University Park, PA: Pennsylvania State University Press.

Delgado, R. (Ed.). (1995). *Critical race theory: The cutting edge*. Philadelphia: Temple University Press.

Delpit, L. D. (1995). *Other people's children: Cultural conflict in the classroom*. New York: New Press.

Delpit, L., & Dowdy, J. K. (2002). *The skin that we speak: Thoughts on language and culture in the classroom*. New York: New Press.

DeNavas-Walt, C., Proctor, B. D., & Lee, C. H. (2005). *Income, poverty, and health insurance coverage in the United States, 2004. U.S. Census Bureau, current population reports*. Series P60-229. Washington, DC: U.S. Government Printing Office.

Dershowitz, A. M. (1997). *The vanishing American Jew: In search of Jewish identity for the next century*. New York: Little, Brown.

Dewey, J. (1959). *Experience and education*. New York: Macmillan.

Dickeman, M. (1973). Teaching cultural pluralism. In J. A. Banks (Ed.), *Teaching ethnic studies: Concepts and strategies* (pp. 5–25). Washington, DC: National Council for the Social Studies.

Dillon, S. (2006, August 27). In schools across U.S., the melting pot overflows. *New York Times, 155* (53,684), A7, 16.

Dorris, M. (1992). *Morning girl*. New York: Hyperion Books for Children.

Douglass, M., & Roberts, G. S. (Eds.). (2000). *Japan and global migration: Foreign workers and the advent of a multicultural society*. London: Routledge.

Drachsler, J. (1920). *Democracy and assimilation*. New York: Macmillan.

Drake, St. C. (1987). *Black folk here and there* (vol. 1). Los Angeles: Center for Afro-American Studies, University of California.

D'Souza, D. (1991). *Illiberal education: The politics of race and sex on campus*. New York: Free Press.

Eck, D. L. (2001). *A new religious America: How a "Christian country" has become the world's most religiously diverse nation*. New York: HarperSanFrancico.

Edelman, M. W. (1992). *The measure of our success: A letter to my children and yours*. Boston: Beacon Press.

Edmonds, R. (1986). Characteristics of effective schools. In U. Neisser (Ed.), *The school achievement of minority children: New perspectives* (pp. 93–104). Hillsdale, NJ: Erlbaum.

Eisen, V., & Hall, I. (Eds.). (1996). Lesbian, gay, bisexual, and transgender people and education. *Harvard Educational Review, 66*(2), 173–435 (special issue).

Ethnomathematics. Retrieved September 10, 2006, from /www.cs.uidaho.edu/~casey931/seminar/ethno.html

Feagin, J. R., & Sikes, M. P. (1994). *Living with racism: The Black middle-class experience.* Boston: Beacon Press.

Ferguson, A. A. (2001). *Bad boys: Public schools in the masking of Black masculinity.* Ann Arbor: University of Michigan Press.

Foner, E. (1998). *The story of American freedom.* New York: Norton.

Ford, D. (1996). *Reversing underachievement among gifted Black students: Promising practices and programs.* New York: Teachers College Press.

Ford, D. Y. (2007). Recruiting and retaining gifted students from diverse ethnic, cultural, and language groups. In J. A. Banks & C. A. M. Banks (Eds.), *Multicultural education: Issues and perspectives* (6th ed., pp. 401–421). Hoboken, NJ: Wiley.

Fordham, S. (1988). Racelessness as a factor in Black students' school success: Pragmatic strategy or pyrrhic victory? *Harvard Educational Review, 58*(1), 54–84.

Franklin, J. H. (1976). *Racial equality in America.* Chicago: University of Chicago Press.

Franklin, J. H. (2005). *Mirror to America: The autobiography of John Hope Franklin.* New York: Farrar, Straus and Giroux.

Franklin, J. H., & Moss, A. A., Jr. (2000). *From slavery to freedom: A history of African Americans* (8th ed.). New York: McGraw-Hill.

Freire, P. (2000). *Pedagogy of the oppressed* (30th anniv. ed.). New York: Continuum.

Friedman, T. L. (2005). *The world is flat: A brief history of the twenty-first century.* New York: Farrar, Straus and Giroux.

García, E. (2005). *Teaching and learning in two languages: Bilingualism and schooling in the United States.* New York: Teachers College Press.

Garcia, R. L. (1993). Prepublication review of the manuscript for 2nd edition of this book: *An introduction to multicultural education.*

Gardner, H. (2006). *Development and education of the mind: The selected works of Howard Gardner.* London & New York: Routledge.

Gates, H. L., Jr., & McKay, N. Y. (Eds.). (1997). *The Norton anthology of African American literature.* New York: Norton.

Gay, G. (2000). *Culturally responsive teaching: Theory, research and practice.* New York: Teachers College Press.

Geary, J., & Graff, J. (2005, Nov. 21). Restless youth: Can France bring order to the streets and hope to the restive minorities of the banlieues? *Time, 166*(21), pp. 24–27.

Geertz, C. (1995). *After the fact: Two countries, four decades, one anthropologist.* Cambridge, MA: Harvard University Press.

Gimmestad, B. J., & DeChiara, E. (1982). Dramatic plays: A vehicle for prejudice reduction in the elementary school. *Journal of Educational Research, 76*(1), 45–49.

Giroux, H. A. (1988). *Teachers as intellectuals: Toward a critical pedagogy of learning.* Granby, MA: Bergin & Garvey.

Glazer, N. (1997). *We are all multiculturalists now.* Cambridge, MA: Harvard University Press.

Golden, R., McConnell, M., Mueller, P., Poppen, C., & Turkovich, M. (1991). *Dangerous memories: Invasion and resistance since 1492.* Chicago: Chicago Religious Task Force on Central America.

Gonçalves e Sliva, P. B. (2004). Citizenship and education in Brazil: The contribution of Indian peoples and Blacks in the struggle for citizenship. In J. A. Banks (Ed.), *Diversity and citizenship education: Global perspectives* (pp. 185–217). San Francisco: Jossey-Bass.

Gonzales, M. G. (1999). *Mexicanos: A history of Mexicans in the United States.* Bloomington: Indiana University Press.

Gonzáles, N., Moll, L. C., & Amanti, C. (Eds.). (2005). *Funds of knowledge: Theorizing practices in households, communities, and classrooms.* Mahwah, NJ: Erlbaum.

Gordon, M. M. (1964). *Assimilation in American life.* New York: Oxford University Press.

Gould, S. J. (1981). *The mismeasure of man.* New York: Norton.

Gould, S. J. (1996). *The mismeasure of man* (rev. & exp. ed). New York: Norton.

Graff, G. (1992). *Beyond the cultural wars: How teaching the conflicts can revitalize American education.* New York: Norton.

Graham, P. A. (2005). *Schooling in America: How the public schools meet the nation's changing needs.* New York: Oxford University Press.

Gray, P. (1991, July 8). Whose America? *Time, 138,* 13–17.

Green, R. L. (2000). *Expectations: How teacher expectations can increase student achievement.* Dillion, CO: Alpine Guild.

Greene, M. (1988). *The dialectic of freedom.* New York: Teachers College Press.

Greeno, J. G., Collins, A. M., & Resnick, L. (1996). Cognition and learning. In D C. Berlinger & R. C. Calfee (Eds.), *Handbook of educational psychology* (pp. 15–46). New York: Macmillan.

Gregorian, G. (2003). *Islam: A mosaic, not a monolith.* Washington, DC: Brookings Institution Press.

Guthrie, J. A. (Ed.). (2003). *Encyclopedia of education* (vol. 8, 2nd ed., pp. 3087–3090). New York: Macmillan Reference USA.

Gutiérrez, R. A. (2004). Ethnic Mexicans in historical and social science scholarship. In J. A. Banks & C. A. M. Banks (Eds.), *Handbook of research on multicultural education* (2nd ed., pp. 261–297). San Francisco: Jossey-Bass.

Gutmann, A. (2003). *Identity in democracy.* Princeton, NJ: Princeton University Press.

Gutmann, A. (2004). Unity and diversity in democratic multicultural education: Creative and destructive tensions. In J. A. Banks (Ed.), *Diversity and citizenship education: Global perspectives* (pp. 71–96). San Francisco: Jossey-Bass.

Harding, S. (1991). *Whose knowledge? Whose science? Thinking from women's lives.* Ithaca, NY: Cornell University Press.

Harding, S. (1998). *Is science multicultural? Postcolonialisms, feminisms, and epistemologies.* Bloomington: Indiana University Press.

Hargreaves, A. G. (1995). *Immigration, "race," and ethnicity in France.* London & New York: Routledge.

Heath, S. B., & McLaughlin, M. W. (Eds.). (1993). *Identity and inner-city youth: Beyond ethnicity and gender.* New York: Teachers College Press.

Hewstone, M., & Brown, R. (1986). Contact is not enough: An intergroup perspective on the "contact hypothesis." In M. Hewstone & R. Brown (Eds.), *Contact and conflict in intergroup encounters* (pp. 1–44). New York: Basil Blackwell.

Hidalgo, N. M., Siu, S-F., & Epstein, J. L. (2004). Research on families, schools, and communities: A multicultural perspective. In J. A. Banks & C. A. M. Banks (Eds.), *Handbook of research on multicultural education* (2nd ed., pp. 631–655). San Francisco: Jossey-Bass.

Hirschfelder, A. (Ed.). (1995). *Native heritage: Personal accounts by American Indians 1790 to the present.* New York: Macmillan.

Hoff, G. (2001). Multicultural education in Germany: Historical development and current trends. In J. A. Banks & C. A. M. Banks (Eds.), *Handbook of research on multicultural education* (pp. 821–838). San Francisco: Jossey-Bass.

Howard, G. R. (2006). *We can't teach what we don't know: White teachers, multicultural schools* (2nd ed.). New York: Teachers College Press.

Howe, I. (1991, February 18). The value of the canon. *New Republic,* 40–44.

Hu-DeHart, E. (2004). Ethnic studies in U.S. higher education: History, development, and goals. In J. A. Banks & C. A. M. Banks (Eds.), *Handbook of research on multicultural education* (2nd ed., pp. 869–881). San Francisco: Jossey-Bass.

Huntington, S. P. (2004). *Who are we? The challenges of America's national identity.* New York: Simon & Schuster.

Hyatt, V. L., & Nettleford, R. (1995). *Race, discourse, and the origin of the Americas: A new world view.* Washington, DC: Smithsonian Institution Press.

Ijaz, M. A., & Ijaz, I. H. (1981). A cultural program for changing racial attitudes. *History and Social Science Teacher, 17*(1), 17–20.

Indianapolis Public Schools. (1996, November). *Resolution No. 7397: Indianapolis Public Schools multicultural education.* Indianapolis: Author.

Irvine, J. J. (2003). *Educating teachers for diversity: Seeing with a cultural eye.* New York: Teachers College Press.

Irvine, J. J., & York, D. E. (1995). Learning styles and culturally diverse students: A literature review. In J. A. Banks & C. A. McGee Banks (Eds.), *Handbook of research on multicultural education* (pp. 484–497). San Francisco: Jossey-Bass.

Jackson, P. (1992). *Untaught lessons.* New York: Teachers College Press.

Jacobson, M. F. (1998). *Whiteness of a different color: European immigrants and the alchemy of race.* Cambridge, MA: Harvard University Press.

Jacoby, S. (2000). *Half-Jew: A daughter's search for her family's buried past.* New York: Scribners.

Jane, L. C. (1989). *The journal of Christopher Columbus.* New York: Bonanza Books.

Josephy, A. M., Jr. (1992). *America in 1492: The world of the Indian peoples before the arrival of Columbus.* New York: Knopf.

Johnson, D. W., & Johnson, R. T. (1981). Effects of cooperative and individual-istic learning experiences on interethnic interaction. *Journal of Educational Psychology, 73,* 444–449.

Johnson, D. W., & Johnson, R. T. (1991). *Learning together and alone* (3rd ed.). Englewood Cliffs, NJ: Prentice-Hall.

Johnson, W. B., & Packer, A. B. (1987). *Workforce 2000: Work and workers for the 21st century.* Washington, DC: U.S. Government Printing Office.

Katz, P. A., & Zalk, S. R. (1978). Modification of children's racial attitudes. *Developmental Psychology, 14,* 447–461.

King, E. W. (2006). *Meeting the challenge of teaching in an era of terrorism.* Mason, OH: Thomson Publishers.

King, M. L. (1987). Selected by C. S. King. *The words of Martin Luther King, Jr.* New York: Newmarket Press.

Kornhaber, M. L. (2004). Assessment, standards, equity. In J. A. Banks & C. A. M. Banks (Eds.), *Handbook of research on multicultural education* (2nd ed., pp. 91–109). San Francisco: Jossey-Bass.

Kymlicka, W. (1995). *Multicultural citizenship: A liberal theory of minority rights.* New York: Oxford University Press.

Kymlicka, W. (2004). Foreword. In J. A. Banks (Ed.), *Diversity and citizenship education: Global perspectives* (pp. xiii–xviii). San Francisco: Jossey-Bass.

Ladson-Billings, G. (1994). *The dreamkeepers: Successful teachers of African American children.* San Francisco: Jossey-Bass.

Ladson-Billings, G. (2001). *Crossing over to Canaan: The journey of new teachers in diverse classrooms.* San Francisco: Jossey-Bass.

Ladson-Billings, G. (2004). New directions in multicultural education: Complexities, boundaries, and critical race theory. In J. A. Banks & C. A. M. Banks (Eds.), *Handbook of research on multicultural education* (2nd ed., pp. 50–65). San Francisco: Jossey-Bass.

Ladson-Billings, G., & Gillborn, D. (Eds.). (2004). *The RoutledgeFalmer Reader in multicultural education.* London & New York: RoutledgeFalmer.

Lee, C. D. (2007). *The role of culture in learning academic literacies: Conducting our blooming in the midst of the whirlwind.* New York: Teachers College Press.

Lee, C. D., & Smagorinsky, P. (Eds.). (2000). *Vygotskian perspectives on literacy research: Constructing meaning through collaborative inquiry.* New York: Cambridge University Press.

Lee, W. O., Grossman, D. L., Kennedy, K. J., & Fairbrother, G. P. (Eds.). (2004). *Citizenship education in Asia and the Pacific: Concepts and issues.* Hong Kong: Comparative Education Research Centre, University of Hong Kong.

Lefkowtiz, M. R., & Rogers, G. M. (1996). *Black Athena revisited.* Chapel Hill & London: The University of North Carolina Press.

Leo, J. (2000). *Incorrect thoughts: Notes on our wayward culture.* Piscataway, NJ: Transaction.

Levine, L. W. (1996). *The opening of the American mind: Canons, culture, and history.* Boston: Beacon.

Levine, L. W., & Lezotte, D. U. (2001). Effective schools research. In J. A. Banks & C. A. M. Banks (Eds.), *Handbook of research on multicultural education* (pp. 525–547). San Francisco: Jossey-Bass.

Levinson, D., & Ember, M. (Eds.). (1996). *Encyclopedia of cultural anthropology* (vol. 1). New York: Holt.

Litcher, J. H., & Johnson, D. W. (1969). Changes in attitudes toward Negroes of White elementary school students after use of multiethnic readers. *Journal of Educational Psychology, 60,* 148–152.

Lightfoot, S. L. (1988). *Balm in Gilead: Journey of a healer.* Reading, MA: Addison Wesley.

Limage, L. J. (2000). Education and Muslim identity: The case of France. *Comparative Education, 36*(1), 73–94.

Limerick, P. N. (1987). *The legacy of conquest: The unbroken past of the American west.* New York: Norton.

Limerick, P. N. (2000). *Something in the social: Legacies and reckonings in the new west.* New York: Norton.

Lipkin, A. (1999). *Understanding homosexuality, changing schools.* Boulder, CO: Westview Press.

Lipman, P. (2004). *High stakes education: Inequality, globalization, and urban school reform.* New York & London: RoutledgeFalmer.

Loewen, J. W. (1995). *Lies my teacher told me: Everything your American history textbook got wrong.* New York: New Press.

Loewen, J. W. (1999). *Lies across America: What our historic sites get wrong.* New York: New Press.

Loewen, J. W. (2005). *Sundown towns: A hidden dimension of American racism.* New York: New Press.

Lubiano, W. (1997). *The house that race built: Black Americans, U.S. terrain.* New York: Pantheon.

Luchtenberg, S. (Ed.). (2004). *Migration, education and change.* London: Routledge.

McNeil, L. M. (2000). *Contradictions of school reform: Educational costs of standardized testing.* New York: Routledge.

Mahiri, J. (2004). *What they don't learn in school: Literacy in the lives of urban youth.* New York: Lang.

Marshall, G. (1994). *The concise Oxford dictionary of sociology.* New York: Oxford University Press.

Martin, P., & Widgren, J. (2002). International migration: Facing the challenge. *Population Bulletin, 57*(1). Washington, DC: Population Reference Bureau.

Martinez, G. M., & Curry, A. E. (1998). *School enrollment: Social and economic characteristics of students (update): October 1998. U.S. Census Bureau, Current Population Reports,* Series P20-521. Washington, DC: U.S. Government Printing Office.

McGoldrick, M., Giordano, J., & Pearce, J. K. (Eds.). (1996). *Ethnicity and family therapy* (2nd ed.). New York: Guilford.

McGregor, J. (1993). Effectiveness of role playing and antiracist teaching in reducing student prejudice. *Journal of Educational Research, 86*(4), 215–226.

Meier, D., & Wood, G. H. (Eds.). (2005). *Many children left behind: How the No Child Left Behind Act is damaging our children and our schools.* Boston: Beacon.

Michigan Department of Education. (1980). *Position statement on multicultural education.* Lansing, MI: Author.

Modood, T., Triandafyllidou, A., & Zapata-Barrero, R. (Eds.). (2006). *Multicultur-alism, Muslims and citizenship: A European approach.* London & New York: Routledge.

Moodley, K. A. (2001). Multicultural education in Canada: Historical development and current status. In J. A. Banks & C. A. M. Banks (Eds.), *Handbook of research on multicultural education* (pp. 801–820). San Francisco: Jossey-Bass.

Morison, S. E. (1974). *The European discovery of America: The southern voyages, 1492–1616.* New York: Oxford University Press.

Moses, R. P., & Cobb, C. E., Jr. (2001). *Radical equations: Math literacy and civil rights.* Boston: Beacon Press.

Muir, K. (1990). Eyes on the Prize: A review. Paper submitted to J. A. Banks as partial requirement for the course EDUC 423, Educating diverse groups. Seattle: University of Washington.

Murphy-Shigematsu, S. (2004). Expanding the borders of the nation: Ethnic diversity and citizenship education in Japan. In J. A. Banks (Ed.), *Diversity and citizenship education: Global perspectives* (pp. 303–332). San Francisco: Jossey-Bass.

Muzzey, D. S. (1915). *Readings in American history.* Boston: Ginn.

Myrdal, G., with Sterner, R., & Rose, A. (1944). *An American dilemma: The Negro problem and modern democracy.* New York: Harper & Row.

Nagda, B. R. A. (2006). Breaking barriers, crossing borders, building bridges: Communication Processes in intergroup dialogues. *Journal of Social Issues, 62*(3), 553–576.

Nasir, N. S., & Cobb, P. (Eds.). (2007). *Improving access to mathematics: Diversity and equity in the classroom.* New York: Teachers College Press.

National Association of Child Care Resource and Referral Agencies (NACCRRA). (2006). *Child care in America.* Retrieved September 9, 2006 from www.naccrra.org/.

National Center for Education Statistics (NCES). (2001, January). *Statistics in brief.* Washington, DC: U.S. Department of Education.

National Center for Education Statistics (NCES). (2006a). Percentage distribution of enrollment in public elementary and secondary schools, by race/ethnicity and state or jurisdiction: fall 1993 and fall 2003. Institute of Education Sciences, U.S. Department of Education. Retrieved August 16, 2006, from http://nces.ed.gov/programs/digest/d05/tables/dt05_038.asp.

National Center for Education Statistics (NCES). (2006b). Student effort and educational progress: Status dropout rates by race/ethnicity: Table 26-2: Status dropout rates and number and percentage distribution of dropouts ages 16–24, by selected characteristics: October 2004. Retrieved August 23, 2006, from http://nces.ed.gov/programs/coe/2006/section3/table.asp?tableID=482.

National Council for the Accreditation of Teacher Education (NCATE). (1997). *Standards for procedures and policies for the accreditation of professional education units.* Washington, DC: Author.

National Council for the Accreditation of Teacher Education (NCATE). (2006). *Professional standards for the accreditation of schools, colleges, and departments of education, 2006 edition.* Washington, DC: Author. Retrieved August 18,

2006, from http://www.ncate.org/documents/standards/unit_stnds_2006. pdf.

National Geographic Society. (1991, October). America before Columbus. *National Geographic, 180*(4), 1–124 (special issue).

National Science Foundation (NSF). (2006). Science and engineering indicators 2006: The rapidly changing global R&D landscape: Some perspectives on U.S. and international S&T growth. Retrieved August 25, 2006, from http://www.nsf.gov/news/news_summ.jsp?cntn_id=105857&org=NSF.

Nebraska Legislature. (1992, January 8). Legislature Bill 922, Final reading. Ninety-Second Legislature, Second Session. Lincoln, NE: Author.

New York (City) Board of Education. (1989). *Statement of policy on multicultural education and promotion of positive intergroup relations.* New York: Author.

Nieto, S. (2004). *Affirming diversity: The sociopolitical context of multicultural education* (4th ed.). Boston: Allyn and Bacon.

Nieto, S. (2005). Public education in the twentieth century and beyond: High hopes, broken promises, and an uncertain future. *Harvard Educational Review, 75*(1), 43–64.

Noguera, P. A. (2003a). *City schools and the American dream: Reclaiming the promise of public education.* New York: Teachers College Press.

Noguera, P. A. (2003b). The trouble with Black boys: The role and influence of environmental and cultural factors on the academic performance of African American males. *Urban Education, 38,* 411–459.

Nott, J. C., & Gliddon, G. R. (Eds.). (1854). *Types of mankind.* Philadelphia, PA: Lippincott, Grambo.

Nussbaum, M. C. (1997). *Cultivating humanity: A classical defense of reform in liberal education.* Cambridge, MA: Harvard University Press.

Nussbaum, M. C. (2002). Patriotism and cosmopolitanism. In J. Cohen (Ed.), *For love of country* (pp. 2–17). Boston: Beacon Press.

Oakes, J. (2005). *Keeping track: How schools structure inequality.* New Haven, CT: Yale University Press.

Olsen, F. (1974). *On the trail of the Arawaks.* Norman: University of Oklahoma Press.

Olson, J. S., & Olson, J. E. (1995). *Cuban Americans: From trauma to triumph.* New York: Twayne.

Orwell, G. (1946). *Animal farm.* New York: Harcourt Brace.

Osler, A. (Ed.). (2000). *Citizenship and democracy in schools: Diversity, identity, equality.* Stoke-on-Trent, UK: Trentham Books.

Osler, A. (Ed.). (2005). *Teachers, human rights, and diversity.* Stoke-on-Trent, UK: Trentham Books.

Painter, N. I. (2005). *Creating Black Americans: African American history and its meanings, 1619 to the present.* New York: Oxford University Press.

Pallas, A. M., Natriello, G., & McDill, E. L. (1989). The changing nature of the disadvantaged population: Current dimensions and future trends. *Educational Researcher, 18,* 16–22.

Parekh, B. (1986). The concept of multi-cultural education. In S. Modgil, G. K. Verma, K. Mallick, & C. Modgil (Eds.), *Multicultural education: The interminable debate* (pp. 19–31). Philadelphia: Falmer Press.

Parekh, B. (2006). *Rethinking multiculturalism: Cultural diversity and political theory* (2nd ed.). New York: Pelgrave Macmillan.

Parker, W. P. (2003). *Teaching democracy: Unity and diversity in public life.* New York: Teachers College Press.

Pellegrino, J. W., Chudowsky, N., & Glaser, R. (Eds.). (2001). *Knowing what students know: The science and design of educational assessment.* Washington, DC: National Academy Press.

Peters, W. (1987). *A class divided: Then and now* (exp. ed.). New Haven, CT: Yale University Press.

Ponce de Leon, J. (1992). The Native American response to the Columbus quincentenary. *Multicultural Review, 1,* 20–22.

Portes, A., & Rumbaut, R. G. (2001). *Legacies: The story of the immigrant second generation.* Berkeley: University of California Press; & New York: Russell Sage Foundation.

Powell, A. B., & Frankenstein, M. (Eds.). (1997). *Ethnomathematics: Challenging Eurocentrism in mathematics education.* Albany: State University of New York.

Ramirez, M., III, & Castaneda, A. (1974). *Cultural democracy, bicognitive development, and education.* New York: Academic Press.

Ravitch, D. (1990). Diversity and democracy: Multicultural education in America. *American Educator, 14,* 16–20 ff. 46–48.

Reich, R. (2002). *Bridging liberalism and multiculturalism in American education.* Chicago: University of Chicago Press.

Reschly, D. J. (1988). Minority MMR overrepresentation and special education reform. *Exceptional Children, 54,* 316, 323.

Richman, L. S. (1990, April 9). The coming world labor shortage. *Fortune,* 70–77.

Roderick, M., Jacob, B. A., & Bryk, A. S. (2002). The impact of high-stakes testing in Chicago on student achievement in promotional gate grades. *Educational Evaluation and Policy Analysis, 24*(4), 333–357.

Rodriguez, R. (1982). *Hunger of memory: The education of Richard Rodriguez.* Boston: Godine.

Roediger, D. R. (2005). *Working toward whiteness: How America's immigrants became White, the journey from Ellis Island to the suburbs.* New York: Basic Books.

Root, M. P. P., & Kelley, M. (Eds.). (2003). *Multiracial child resource book: Living complex identities.* Seattle, WA: Mavin Foundation.

Rosaldo, R. (1997). Cultural citizenship, inequality, and multiculturalism. In W. V. Florres & R. Benmayor (Eds.), *Latino cultural citizenship: Claiming identity, space, and rights* (pp. 27–28). Boston: Beacon.

Rothenberg, P. S. (Ed.). (2000). *Race, class, and gender in the United States: An integrated study* (5th ed.). New York: Worth.

Rothstein, R. (2004). *Class and schools: Using social, economic, and educational reform to close the Black-White achievement gap.* New York: Teachers College, Columbia University, Economic Policy Institute.

Rouse, I. (1992). *The Tainos: Rise and decline of the people who greeted Columbus.* New Haven, CT: Yale University Press.

Schlesinger, A. (1991). *The disuniting of America: Reflections on a multicultural society.* Knoxville, TN: Whittle Direct Books.

Schmitz, B., Butler, J. E., Guy-Sheftall, B., & Rosenfelt, D. (2004). Women's studies and curriculum transformation in the United States. In J. A. Banks & C. A. M. Banks (Eds.), *Handbook of research on multicultural education* (2nd ed., pp. 882–905). San Francisco: Jossey-Bass.

Secada, W. G., Fennema, E., & Adajian, L. B. (Eds.). (1995). *New directions for equity in mathematics education.* New York: Cambridge University Press.

Sen, A. (2006). *Identity and violence: The illusion of destiny.* New York: Norton.

Shirts, G. (1969). *Starpower.* LaJolla, CA: Western Behavioral Science Institute. This game is now available from Simulation Training Systems, P.O. Box 910, Del Mar, CA 92014. Telephone: 800-942-2900 or 858-755-0272. Website: http://www.stsintl.com/business/index.html.

Schofield, J. W. (2001). Improving intergroup relations. In J. A. Banks & C. A. M. Banks (Eds.), *Handbook of research on multicultural education* (pp. 635–646). San Francisco: Jossey-Bass.

Schuman, H., Steeh, C., Bobo, L., & Krysan, M. (1997). *Racial attitudes in America: Trends and interpretations* (rev. ed.). Cambridge, MA: Harvard University Press.

Sen, A. (2006). *Identity and violence: The illusion of destiny.* New York: Norton.

Sertima, I. V. (1984). *Black women in antiquity.* New Brunswick, NJ: Transaction Books.

Shin, H. B., with Bruno, R. (2003). *Language use and English-speaking ability: 2000.* Washington, DC: U.S. Census Bureau. Retrieved August 16, 2006, from http://www.census.gov/prod/2003pubs/c2kbr-29.pdf.

Sirkin, G. (1990, January 18). The multi-culturalists strike again. *Wall Street Journal,* p. A14.

Slavin, R. E. (1979). Effects of biracial learning teams on cross-racial friendships. *Journal of Educational Psychology, 71,* 381–387.

Slavin, R. E. (1983). *Cooperative learning.* New York: Longman.

Slavin, R. E. (1985). Cooperative learning: Applying contact theory in desegregated schools. *Journal of Social Issues, 41,* 45–62.

Slavin, R. E. (2001). Cooperative learning and intergroup relations. In J. A. Banks & C. A. M. Banks (Eds.), *Handbook of research on multicultural education* (pp. 628–634). San Francisco: Jossey-Bass.

Slavin, R. E, & Madden, N. A. (1979). School practices that improve race relations. *American Educational Research Journal, 16*(2), 169–180.

Slavin, R. E., & Madden, N. A. (2001). *One million children: Success for all.* Thousand Oaks, CA: Corwin Press.

Sleeter, C. E. (2005). *Un-standardizing curriculum: Multicultural teaching in the standards-based classroom.* New York: Teachers College Press.

Sleeter, C. E., & Grant, C. A. (1991). Race, class, gender, and disability in current textbooks. In M. W. Apple & L. K. Christian-Smith (Eds.), *The politics of the textbook* (pp. 78–110). New York: Routledge.

Sleeter, C. E., & Grant, C. A. (1997). An analysis of multicultural education in the United States. *Harvard Educational Review, 7,* 421–444.

Smitherman, G. (2000). *Talkin that talk: Language, culture, and education in African America.* New York: Routledge.

Snipp, C. M. (2004). American Indian studies. In J. A. Banks & C. A. M. Banks (Eds.), *Handbook of research on multicultural education* (2nd ed., pp. 315–331). San Francisco: Jossey-Bass.

Solomos, J. (2003). *Race and racism in Britain* (3rd ed.). New York: Pelgrave Macmillan.

Stannard, D. E. (1992). *American holocaust: Columbus and the conquest of the new world.* New York: Oxford University Press.

Statistics Canada. (2000). Report on ethnic origins. Retrieved December 12, 2001, from www.statcan.ca.

Stephan, W. G. (1985). Intergroup relations. In G. Lindzey & E. Aronson (Eds.), *The handbook of social psychology* (vol. 2, 3rd ed., pp. 599–658). New York: Random House.

Stephan, W. G. (1999). *Reducing prejudice and stereotyping in schools.* New York: Teachers College Press.

Stephan, W. G., & Stephan, C. W. (2004). Intergroup relations in multicultural education programs. In J. A. Banks & C. A. M. Banks (Eds.), *Handbook of research on multicultural education* (2nd ed., pp. 782–799). San Francisco: Jossey-Bass.

Stephan, W. G., & Vogt, W. P. (Eds.). (2004). *Education programs for improving intergroup relations: Theory, research, and practice.* New York: Teachers College Press.

Stipek, D. (Chair). (2004). *Engaging schools: Fostering high school students' motivation to learn.* Washington, DC: National Academies Press.

Stone, R. (2004). *Islamophobia: Issues, challenges and action: A report by the Commission on British Muslims and Islamophobia.* Stoke-on-Trent, UK: Trentham Books.

Stotsky, S. (1999). *Losing our language: How multicultural classroom instruction is undermining our children's ability to read, write, and reason.* New York: Free Press.

Stritikus, T., & Varghese, M. M. (2007). Language diversity and schooling. In J. A. Banks & C. A. M. Banks (Eds.), *Multicultural education: Issues and perspectives* (6th ed., pp. 297–325). Hoboken, NJ: Wiley.

Sue, D. W. (2004). Multicultural counseling and therapy (MCT) theory. In J. A. Banks & C. A. M. Banks (Eds.), *Handbook of research on multicultural education* (2nd ed., pp. 813–827). San Francisco: Jossey-Bass.

Taba, H., Brady, E., & Robinson, J. (1952). *Intergroup education in public schools.* Washington, DC: American Council on Education.

Taba, H., Durkin, M. C., Fraenkel, J., & McNaughton, A. N. (1971). *A teacher's handbook to elementary social studies: An inductive approach* (2nd ed.). Reading, MA: Addison-Wesley.

Takaki, R. (1989). *Strangers from a different shore: A history of Asian Americans.* Boston: Little, Brown.

Takaki, R. (1993). *A different mirror: A history of multicultural America.* Boston: Little, Brown.

Takaki, R. (1998). *A larger memory: A history of our diversity, with voices.* New York: Little, Brown.

Telles, E. E. (2004). *Race in another America: The significance of skin color in Brazil.* Princeton, NJ: Princeton University Press.

Tomlinson, S. (2001). *Education in a post-welfare society.* Buckingham, UK, & Philadelphia: Open University Press.

Toossi, M. (2002). A century of change: The U.S. labor force, 1950–2050. *Monthly Labor Review, 125*(5), 15–28.

Toossi, M. (2005). Labor force projections to 2014: Retiring boomers. *Monthly Labor Review, 128*(11), 25–44.

Trager, H. G., & Yarrow, M. R. (1952). *They learn what they live: Prejudice in young children.* New York: Harper.

Treisman, U. (1992). Studying students studying calculus: A look at the lives of minority mathematics students in college. *College Mathematics Journal, 23*(5), 362–372.

University of Washington, Office of the Registrar. (2006, spring). *Quarterly enrollment profile.* Seattle: Author.

U.S. Census Bureau. (2000). *Statistical abstract of the United States: 2000* (120th ed.). Washington, DC: U.S. Government Printing Office.

U.S. Census Bureau. (2003, October). *Language use and English-speaking ability: 2000.* (H. B. Shin with R. Bruno). Washington, DC: U.S. Government Printing Office.

U.S. Census Bureau. (2004). Population profile of the United States: Dynamic version: Poverty in 2004. Retrieved August 28, 2006, from http://www.census.gov/population/pop-profile/dynamic/poverty.pdf.

U.S. Census Bureau. (2004). The foreign-born population in the United States: 2003: Population characteristics. Retrieved August 25, 2006, from http://www.census.gov/prod/2004pubs/p20-551.pdf.

U.S. Census Bureau. (2006a). *Annual estimates of the population by sex, race and Hispanic or Latino origin for the United States: April 1, 2000, to July 1, 2005* (NC-EST2005-03). Washington, DC: U.S. Government Printing Office.

U.S. Census Bureau. (2006b). U.S. interim projections by age, sex, race, and Hispanic origin: Table 1b: Projected population change in the United States, by race and Hispanic origin: 2000 to 2050. Retrieved August 25, 2006, from http://www.census.gov/ipc/www/usinterimproj/natprojtab01b.pdf.

U.S. Department of Education, Institute of Education Services. (1993, fall; 2003, fall). Percentage distribution of enrollment in pubic elementary and secondary schools, by race/ethnicity and state or jurisdiction. Retrieved August 16, 2006, from http://nces.ed.gov/programs/digest/d05/tables/dt05_038asp.

U.S. Department of Labor. (2006). Civilian labor force 16 and older by sex, age, race, and Hispanic origin: Table 1: Civilian labor force by sex, age, race, and Hispanic origin, 1984, 1994, 2004, and projected 2014. Retrieved August 25, 2006, from http://www.bls.gov/emp/emplab01.htm.

Valdés, G. (2001). *Learning and not learning English: Latino students in American schools.* New York: Teachers College Press.

Valenzuela, A. (1999). *Substractive schooling: U.S.–Mexican youth and the politics of caring.* Albany: State University of New York Press.

Van Ausdale, D., & Feagin, J. R. (2001). *The first r: How children learn race and racism.* Lanham, MD: Rowman & Littlefield.

Wardle, F., & Cruz-Janzen, M. I. (2004). *Meeting the needs of multiethnic and multi-racial children in schools.* Boston: Allyn and Bacon.

Weatherford, J. (1988). *Indian givers: How the Indians of the Americas transformed the world.* New York: Fawcett Columbine.

Weatherford, J. (1991). *Native roots: How the Indians enriched America.* New York: Fawcett Columbine.

Weiner, M. J., & Wright, F. E. (1973). Effects of undergoing arbitrary discrimination upon subsequent attitudes toward a minority group. *Journal of Applied Social Psychology, 3,* 94–102.

West, C. (2004). *Democracy matters: Winning the fight against imperialism.* New York: Penguin.

White, J. L., & Parham, T. A. (1990). *The psychology of Blacks: An African-American perspective* (2nd ed.). Englewood Cliffs, NJ: Prentice-Hall.

Wiggins, G., & McTighe, J. (1998). *Understanding by design.* Alexandria, VA: Association for Supervision and Curriculum Development.

Williams, R. M. (1947). *Reduction of intergroup tensions.* New York: Social Science Research Council.

Willis, P. (1977). *Learning to labor: How working class kids get working class jobs.* New York: Columbia University Press.

Wilson, W. J. (1999). *The bridge over the racial divide: Rising inequality and coalition politics.* Berkeley: University of California Press; & New York: Russell Sage Foundation.

Wong Fillmore, L. (2005). When learning a second language means losing the first. In M. M. Suárez-Orozco, C. Suárez-Orozco, & D. B. Quin (Eds.), *The new immigration: An interdisciplinary reader* (pp. 289–307). New York & London: Routledge.

Wood, P. B., & Sonleitner, N. (1996). The effect of childhood interracial contact on adult anti-Black prejudice. *International Journal of Intercultural Relations, 20*(1), 1–17.

Wright, M. A. (1998). *I'm chocolate, you're vanilla: Raising healthy Black and biracial children in a race-conscious world.* San Francisco: Jossey-Bass.

Yawkey, T. D., & Blackwell, J. (1974). Attitudes of 4-year-old urban Black children toward themselves and Whites based upon multi-ethnic social studies materials and experiences. *Journal of Educational Research, 67,* 373–377.

Young, I. M. (2000). *Inclusion and democracy.* New York: Oxford University Press.

Zinn, H. (2001). *Howard Zinn on history.* New York: Seven Stories Press.

Credits

James A. Banks, "Approaches to Multicultural Curriculum Reform." *Multicultural Leader*, vol. 1, no. 2 (Spring, 1988), pp. 1–3; James A. Banks, "Multicultural Education: Development, Dimensions, and Challenges." *Phi Delta Kappan*, vol. 75, no. 1 (Sept. 1993), pp. 22–28; James A. Banks, "Multicultural Literacy and Curriculum Reform." *Educational Horizons*, vol. 69, no. 3 (Spring, 1991), pp. 135–140; James A. Banks, *Multiethnic Education: Practices and Promises*. Bloomington, IN: Phi Delta Kappa Educational Foundation, 1977. Revised with a new bibliography, 1988. James A. Banks, "Reducing Prejudice in Children: Guidelines from Research." *Social Studies and the Young Learner*, vol. 5, no. 2 (Nov./Dec. 1992), pp. 3–5; James A. Banks, *Preparing Teachers and Administrators in a Multicultural Society*. Austin, TX: Southwest Educational Development Laboratory, 1990; "Essential Principles for Teaching and Learning in a Multicultural Society," in J. A. Banks, P. Cookson, G. Gay, W. D. Hawley, J. J. Irvine, S. Nieto, J. W. Schofield, & W. G. Stephan (2001), *Diversity within Unity: Essential Principles for Teaching and Learning in a Multicultural Society*. Seattle: Center for Multicultural Education, University of Washington. Reprinted with permission of the Center for Multicultural Education; James A. Banks, "Multicultural Education: For Freedom's Sake." *Educational Leadership*, vol. 49, no. 1 (Dec. 1991/Jan. 1992), pp. 32–36. Reprinted in revised form with the permission of the Association for Supervision and Curriculum Development; an adapted version of Figure 1, page 8, of James A. Banks (Ed.) (2004), *Diversity and Citizenship Education: Global Perspectives*. San Francisco: Jossey-Bass. Reprinted with permission of John Wiley & Sons; adapted sections from James A. Banks (2002), "Teaching for Diversity and Unity in a Democratic Multicultural Society," in Walter C. Parker (Ed.), *Education for Democracy: Contexts, Curricula, Assessments* (pp. 131–150). Reprinted with permission of Information Age Publishing, Inc.; James A. Banks, with Sam L. Sebesta, *We Americans: Our History and People*, Vol. 1. Boston: Allyn and Bacon, 1982, pp. 35–43; selections from *The Journal of Christopher Columbus* by Anthony Blond. Copyright 1960 by Clarkson N. Potter, Inc. Reprinted by permission of Clarkson N. Potter/Publishers, a division of Random House, Inc.

Index

Page numbers followed by an *f* or *t* indicate figures and tables.